A Vindication of the

Government of

New England Churches

By John Wise

Published by Pantianos Classics

ISBN-13: 978-1-78987-533-1

First published in 1717

Contents

Introduction

The sky of American literature, as now critically surveyed and evaluated, is astonishingly populated with writers who shine in it only after having for some time been eclipsed. Herman Melville is, of course, the recovered star of greatest magnitude, but John Wise is also a luminary with a recently won place in the literary galaxy.

Never quite so lost from memory as Melville, Wise was viewed not as a writer but as an ecclesiastical disputant. The two books which insure his same are *The Churches Quarrel Espoused,* first printed in New York in 1713 and then at Boston in 1715, and *A Vindication of the Government of New-England Churches,* Boston, 1717. Both these were attacks upon *Proposals* for five changes in the ecclesiastical polity practised in eastern Massachusetts. Since the *Proposals* made no headway, the Congregational communities thought of Wise as one who helped maintain the purity of the primitive "New England Way." In 1772, when there was another commotion in the Massachusetts churches, supporters of the pure polity again issued the *Vindication;* in 1860 the Congregational Board of Publication brought out both the *Quarrel* and the *Vindication.* In all these years it occurred to nobody that the books had any interest beyond their ecclesiastical thesis. Moses Coit Tyler was thought eccentric when in 1897 he called Wise probably the most brilliant prose writer of the colonial time (*History of American Literature,* II, 104); not until Vernon L. Partington joyously hailed him in 1927 (*Main Currents in American Thought,* I, 118-125) as the neglected prophet of rural American democracy did opinion suddenly recognize in him the classic he now seems securely to be.

Part of the explanation for this curious history is that Wise's two books actually played no part in the defeat of the *Proposals* of 1705; in eastern Massachusetts these had fallen dead, so that though Wise somewhat annoyed their author, Cotton Mather, he attracted very little attention. Because public opinion was not aroused, few of his contemporaries read him; none realized that here was, in the guise of maintaining the status quo in the churches, a shift in the tactics of defense which is a breath-taking radicalism.

The founders of the colony of Massachusetts Bay in 1630 migrated under the authority of a royal charter; this enabled them in effect to say, or to pretend, that they transported to the wilderness a portion of the English Established Church, and here reformed their piece of it into a pattern of "primitive" Christianity which could then serve as the model for the purification of what was left of the Church at home. These Puritans had no sense of being a peculiar denomination. But history moved faster than they anticipated, in ways which seemed to them perverse, so that by the end of the seventeenth century Massachusetts and Connecticut were possessed of what had been designed as the model of universal reformation, but which was in fact only their peculiar mode of worship. By then they learned, at first reluctantly, later with pride, to call this method "Congregational," and so to think of themselves as no longer Anglicans but as Congregationalists. In this process we can trace the emergence of a colonial as distinct from a national consciousness. But events in the seventeenth century, especially the intestinal fights among the Puritans after they defeated the Royalists, had made crystal clear that the New England Way was opposed not only to the episcopal hierarchy of the Established Church but also to the Presbyterian form which prevailed in Scotland and which the majority of English Nonconformists held to be the true Biblical polity.

The peculiar essence of the Congregational doctrine was the requirement that each "particular" church be founded on a covenant of all those qualified for membership, and that therefore each church be autonomous. New England's formulation of this plan, *The Cambridge Platform* of 1648, made provision for occasional meetings in such synods as the one that drew up that document; it urged the churches to seek advice and council from one another. But Congregationalists allowed no compulsive power over and above each church, neither bishop nor Presbyterian classis or assembly. Upon this proposition the revered founders in the generation of Cotton, Hooker, and Richard Mather had been explicit.

In order to explain their delicate and hazardous rejection of both hierarchies, either of bishops or of presbyters, the clerical leaders wrote many learned treatises, which they sent to London for publication, so that by 1650 or 1660 there existed a vast, weighty, apologetical literature. Richard Mather's *Church-Government and*

Church-Covenant Discussed (1643) was esteemed even by Presbyterian foes; the acknowledged masterpiece of them all was Thomas Hooker's *A Survey of the Summe of Church-Discipline* (1648). In their many writings on behalf of New England in the last decades of the seventeenth century, Increase and Cotton Mather firmly aligned themselves with the philosophy of the fathers and denounced any deviation as treason.

These tracts on polity are the work of men highly trained in the logic of the schools. There is never the slightest suggestion among them that the faculty of reason should not be employed in determining the divinely appointed method. The ground on which they stood, upon which they erected their logical structures, is the authority of the New Testament. They maintained that, by proper reading of the Epistles, by careful unfolding of the implications of specific texts, they could prove that the Congregational, and only the Congregational, method was established by Christ and the Apostles. If these tomes exalt the power of logic it is only in terms of the original Calvinist paradox that reason can be exalted because Scripture is an authoritarian check upon an abuse of reason. But the founders never for a moment conceded that reason itself, either from its own resources or by unaided study of nature, could derive any first principles of ecclesiastical polity. Widely as they used the faculty, they confined it to drawing inferences from the Bible.

Their enemies soon were accusing the Congregationalists' platform of being "democratical." This tendency, Presbyterians felt, was proof of a misapplication of logic. The apologists had a difficult time, but to their own satisfaction were convinced that they refuted the charge: while a particular congregation did come into being by covenanting among the members, and did elect its own officers and administer its own censures, still the rule of the Bible over all of them (and the power of the ministers in interpreting the fundamental law) was so conclusive that there was nothing democratic about the procedure. Or if there was, that element was harmless. One of the apologists succinctly characterized the plan as a speaking aristocracy in the face of a silent democracy. In the original program the emphasis was upon the silence and submission of the covenanted laity. The revocation of the Massachusetts charter in 1684 deprived the order of the support of the civil arm. In the confusions of the arbitrary rule of Sir Edmund Andros in 1685-1689, it became evident that the independence of the congregations encouraged centrifugality. Though under the new charter, which Increase Mather negotiated from William and Mary in 1691, the "standing order" was favored, clear-eyed observers began to wonder if perhaps the founders had not been too naive, that the churches had to be brought under some sort of Presbyterian — or "semi-Presbyterian" — centralization.

The clearest-eyed of all these was the Reverend Solomon Stoddard of Northampton. A massive figure, who dominated that then far and wild West, he organized the clergy of his area into an "Association" which in effect functioned as a classis, and by 1700 he proclaimed the notion of church covenant a mistake. Increase and Cotton Mather united against him in a bitter pamphlet war, which lasted from 1700 to 1710 and ended in a draw, or rather in Stoddard's maintaining his empire in the West. Against him the Mathers argued an absolute duty of loyalty to the platform of the founders. As a maneuver in this resistance, Cotton Mather in 1700 got the two oldest ministers in the colony — John Higginson and William Hubbard, then in their eighties and whose memories went back to the days of John Cotton and Thomas Hooker — to compose as a preface to one of his publications "A Testimony To the Order of the Gospel, in the Churches of New-England." This statement was, therefore, designed to be a Matherian weapon.

It is a bit obscure as to just what Cotton Mather thought he was doing, but the most reasonable explanation — though reason may find itself glimmering when trying to account for Cotton Mather — is that, even while aiding his father in the fight against Stoddard, he saw the cogency of Stoddard's argument of how, in the confusion of 1700, the churches did need at least some degree of co-ordination. At any rate, he was the leading spirit in the formation of an "association" consisting of ministers within the Boston-Cambridge area. From this body, on November 5, 1705 (which he forgot to notice was Guy Fawkes' Day), came the *Proposals*. Compared with what Stoddard had enacted in the Valley, they were mild. They asked that other regions in Massachusetts form similar associations and allow such organizations a surveillance over the election by churches of new ministers, and that these groups review any church's administration of censures or any conflicts (of which there was an increasing number) between people and pastors. The most extravagant of the *Proposals* asked that churches which refused to submit to such arbitration be declared by the association, or consociation, no longer fit for communication with the others.

In Massachusetts, as I say, nothing came of the *Proposals*. Not so much because there was any rooted adherence to the "Independency" of the founders, but simply because there was no incentive for setting up the machinery of association. In Connecticut, where the churches were already looking for leadership to Stoddard rather than to Increase Mather, the colonial government acted; the result in 1708 was *The Saybrook Platform,* which for the rest of the century formed Connecticut's congregation into regional consociations and so created in that colony, even into the time it became a state, a "semi-Presbyterian" system. But eastern Massachusetts was too far gone into individualism. Wise did not need to fight the *Proposals:* he just chose to do so.

Had we no other evidence than the texts of the books, no other insights into the personality of John Wise, we should see that they are extravagant utterances, the more rollicking because the author knows he is flogging a dead horse. Or, to change the metaphor into one he would enjoy, he is a dog gnawing a bone. *The Churches Quarrel Espoused,* which he called a "satyre," is constructed as though a court-orator arraigning an accused is appealing to a jury of solid countrymen with the imagery of farm life — of crops and bees. In all the ministerial literature of New England, since the magisterial founding, there had been nothing like it, except perhaps for Nathaniel Ward's *Simple Cobbler;* yet that was different, because Ward's extravagant style, imitated the baroque luxuriance of Elizabethan writing. Wise's hyperbole and understatement came wholly from the soil of rustic, contemporary Massachusetts; his humor and irony point forward to Thoreau, not backward to the scholastic wit of the first Puritans.

The sort of homage which Parrington and his followers paid to the common man emphasized in the ""rediscovered" figure of John Wise the fact that his father had come to New England as an indentured servant. So here, at least, is one cleric who came not of the ministerial elite, whose progenitor in America was neither a Mather nor a Cotton. He was born in Roxbury in 1652, after his father had served out the indenture, and somehow he went through Harvard College, graduating in the class of 1673. He served as minister at Branford, Connecticut, from 1673 to 1677, and was tried out at Hatfield for another three years. Thus he spent his apprenticeship in the kingdom of Solomon Stoddard, and there he may have learned to hate the slightest token of Presbyterianism. In 1676 he saw brief service with the troops in the war against King Philip.

In the spring of 1680 he was invited to be minister of what was called "Chebacco parish" — a subsidiary of Ipswich township in Essex county (the area is now called Essex). It was not until February, 1682, that this communion could secure its Congregational independence of Ipswich and so officially install Wise as pastor. He served this rustic society, with evident satisfaction, until his death on April 8, 1725. Not a single shred survives of what he preached on any doctrinal subject, though obviously he must have expounded routine Puritan doctrine on every Sabbath: what does endure are legends about his immense prowess as a wrestler.

Chebacco was not, as we measure distance, far from Boston, the metropolis of New England. But in Wise's day it was emphatically rural, far off even the thin highroad from Boston to Portsmouth. Wise might have been, and as far as we can figure was, content to live there in obscurity, had not events forced him to declare himself. The occasions which summoned him from his bucolic serenity before the *Proposals* have by now been chronicled at length, but they bear repeating.

Though Chebacco became in 1682 a distinct church, it remained part of Ipswich township. Wherefore Wise Spoke up at town-meeting in 1687 against Andres's levy of taxes: the record says that he told the people that they "had a good God, & a good King, and Should Do Well to Stand for their previledges." Andros imprisoned him. As a reward for his heroism, the liberated colony assigned him to be chaplain for the mishandled attack on Quebec in 1690; a report survives in which he wrote some scathing reflections on the incompetent generalship. He befriended one of the accused witches; he supported the cause of inoculation against the smallpox; and in his last years he wrote for the Boston press some vehement passages in favor of paper money.

These are his few, his far-between, appearances in public. Few though they be, they add up: we have an unforgettable spokesman, humorous, large, passionate, for the country population of New

England. In his wit, his self-possession, his resolution. Wise seems at every point a complete opposite to the neurotic Cotton Mather. There is, we have been told, a heritage from Puritanism which is inward-gnawing, self-distrustful, morbid; of this Cotton Mather is the epitome. There is another: earthy, skeptical, quite prepared to fight for principle but still more prepared to discount its own motives: we make out a prefiguration — indeed a fairly complete realization — of this strain in the personality and especially in the prose of John Wise.

There may still be a question — which I shall not here pursue — whether this big, easy-going wrestler of a preacher did not suffer from his peculiar bitings-'of the New England conscience, and so doggedly fought against Cotton Mather's *Proposals* long after they were shown to be idiotic. Or maybe he had a grudge to work off. This much is sure: after the high ridicule of the *Quarrel,* he felt compelled to moderate his tone and to refute the stupid *Proposals* by a forensic argument. To our appreciative eyes he appears as the one expounder of Congregational polity who had the courage, and the perception, to present it as a resolutely *democratic polity* — treating the membership as by no means "silent." But when we see how adroitly he managed his presentation, especially how he combined with his references to such founders as John Cotton, Thomas Hooker, and Richard Mather the arguments which both Increase and Cotton Mather had lately been advancing against Solomon Stoddard, we appreciate how maliciously he was constructing his plea for democracy. This minister of the gospel was striving, in every sentence of the *Vindication,* to transfer the whole Congregational position from Biblical authority to the sanction of pure reason. He was so concerned to put the whole issue on a secular ground that even in his Demonstration III, "From Holy Scripture," he elaborately contrived that the ancient proof-texts from the New Testament have to be taken in a rationalistic, civil context.

This is the real achievement of the *Vindication.* We may wonder if Parrington did not somewhat obscure it by hailing Wise as the "village democrat" and so put all the emphasis upon a political moral which may well be in the book but which is secondary to its primary intention. Wise was addressing himself exclusively to the issue raised by the *Proposals,* and was fighting to maintain a way of life which ordinary New Englanders had made their own. However widely he ranged for his arguments, he contracted them all to a single demand: "no interference!" The modern appreciation concentrates upon the second demonstration (pp. 30-70), that from "the Light of Nature." Assuredly this was a bold device: to suppose even for a moment that the Biblical polity *might* have been learned exclusively from natural tuition! However, when we take the work as a whole, we see that this is primarily a strategic maneuver, a feint, in a subtly planned battle against the "Enemy," rather than a full-fledged assertion of eighteenth-century rationalism or a preliminary draft of the Declaration of Independence. Still, the great point all the way through is that both out of reason and out of Christianity, by appealing to both the Puritan conception of history and New England's provincial experience he does vindicate the democratic principle — at least, that is, in church government. In this respect we can indeed assert that there is nothing like his among the utterances of his contemporaries and that there would be none like his in America until the Revolution.

Neither upon the thinking of that crisis nor upon its eloquence did he have an appreciable direct influence; we must be cautious about attributing to him a social philosophy analogous to his ecclesiastical doctrine. But this need not in the slightest hinder us from perceiving his prophetic significance.

For the content of his second demonstration Wise relied heavily upon an English translation (1710) of Baron Samuel Pufendorf's *De Jure Naturae et Gentium* (first published in 1672). A few of his paragraphs are substantial paraphrases. (Wise appears to have been entirely unaware of Locke.) But even when he borrowed, he inserted twists of his own, colloquialisms that come from the New England community. And his blanket assertion of the superiorities of democracy over both monarchy and aristocracy is not Pufendorf's; it is pure Wise.

By 1717 Higginson had been dead eight years and Hubbard for thirteen; their memory was profoundly revered. So we appreciate Wise's cunning, and get another insight into the man, when we find him appending to his treatise the "Testimony" Cotton Mather had in 1700 extracted from this "Venerable Authority." The document suited his malicious purpose all the more because Higginson and Hubbard had, in order to compliment Cotton Mather, added to their own statement a passage from Mather's life of his grandfather, John

Cotton of most blessed memory, a passage which Mather had reprinted in the *Magnalia* of 1702. In his gloating panegyric to these departed saints (p. 105) Wise conveys his glee over the chance to hoist Cotton Mather with Mather's own petard.

In the over-all design of the *Vindication,* wherein the second demonstration may be seen in perspective, what will strike the reader is the forensic skill. The uses of Increase Mather (who had not signed the *Proposals*) as on pages 9, 28, 89, will be seen, as we might say, to be skilfully "planted." And likewise are all Wise's invocations of the founders of New England, before whose mighty images Cotton Mather had prostrated himself in the *Magnalia*. Even more extravagantly than Cotton Mather had dared to do, Wise equates the system of New England, the pure system of the founders, with uncorrupted Christianity. He so contrives his presentation that Mather's feeble *Proposals* are bound to appear the first treasonable steps, in this open country, not toward Presbyterianism but toward popery.

Above all, the *Vindication* is a lively book. It is the pioneer achievement of rationalism in America, but it is always *argumentum ad hominem*. Although "Wise wrote with an awareness that "the Enemy is fairly Vanquished," he reveled in pillorying the *Proposals* as a scheme of despotism (p. 65) and as a plot for cheating the Reformation (p. 66). He hugely enjoyed himself. He was a man of the people. He spoke in the name of the people and it was to them that he addressed his book, not to his learned colleagues in the ministry or to his fellow Harvard graduates.

All the available information about Wise's biography is in George Allan Cook, *John Wise: Early American Democrat* (New York, 1952). I endeavored to set him in relation to the thought of his time in *The New England Mind: From Colony to Province* (Cambridge, 1953). See also, Richard M. Gummere, "John Wise, A Classical Controversialist," *Essex Institute Historical Collections,* XCII (June, 1956), 265-278.

Perry Miller

Harvard University

A VINDICATION

OF THE

Government of *New-England*

Churches.

Drawn from Antiquity ; the Light of
Nature ; Holy Scripture ; its Noble
Nature ; and from the Dignity Di-
vine Providence has put upon it.

By *John Wife* A. M.
Paſtor to a Church in *Ipſwich*.

---

*There is none to guide her among all the Sons
whom ſhe hath brought forth ; neither
is there any that taketh her by the hand
of all the Sons that ſhe hath brought
up,* Iſa. 51. 18.
Say ye unto your Brethren Ammi, *and to
your Siſters* Ruhamah, Hoſ. 2. 1.

BOSTON, Printed by *J. Allen,* for *N.
Boone,* at the Sign of the BIBLE in
Cornhill, 1 7 1 7.

Original title page, 1717

A Vindication of the Government of New-England Churches

Drawn from Antiquity; the Light of Nature; Holy Scripture; its Noble Nature; and from the Dignity Divine Providence has put upon it.

By John Wise A. M. Pastor to a Church in Ipswich

There is none to guide her among all the Sons whom she hath brought forth; neither is there any that taketh her by the hand of all the Sons that she hath brought up, Isa. 51. 18.

Say ye unto your Brethren Ammi, *and to your Sisters* Ruhamah, Hos. 2. 1.

BOSTON, Printed by *J. Allen,* for N. Boone, at the Sign of the BIBLE in *Cornhill,* 1717.

The Constitution of *New-England* CHURCHES, as settled by their Platform, may be fairly Justified, from *Antiquity;* The *Light of Nature; Holy Scripture;* and from the *Noble* and *Excellent Nature* of the *Constitution* it self. And lastly from the *Providence of God* dignifying of it.

I. The first Demonstration contains the Voice of *Antiquity* in the following Chapters,

Chap. I

To Distribute the whole Christian Aera *into three Parts may serve to Raise a Clearer Light, and make a Brighter Aspect in this Essay.*

I. THE first Division contains the first Three hundred years of Christianity, which may be accounted the mod Refined and purest Time, both as to Faith and Manners, that the Christian Church has been Honoured with; for that within this space, is contained the Ministry of the *Apostles* and Holy *Evangelists* and other Eminent persons Authorized by them; and such others who succeeded in Office-Trust through the several Ages, within the space before named. This was the time of an Immense Effusion of the Spirit of God upon the World, when there was such a Flux and Inundation of the Waters from the Sanctuary, mentioned, *Ezek.* 47. This was the Age of Miracles; A time of Extraordinary Gifts, and when Grace and true Piety was in the greatest Elevation. Christian Religion was now a Dangerous Business; Every Man that took it up, lays down his Life, Honour and Fortune at Stake; He that owns Christ, must bid defiance to all the Celebrated Deities of the Roman Empire; and thereby Run Counter to the Religion of the Imperial Court. So that Rationally we may expect to find the Churches of Christ in the purest Capacity they were ever in; In all points, both of Principles and Practice. That whatever their Government was if they continue the same from the days of the Apostles, we may fairly conclude it to be Authentick, and Agreeable with their Grand & Original Copy. It is most Apparent, that the Churches in those Ages, were under too good an Influence Internally, and the Eye of too direful a guard, essentially to prevaricate with God in the known Principles of their Order, any more then in their Faith, tho' they were not without Errors. Two or three hundred years, is a long time in the World, to keep up our constant Mode, and Custome, either in Religious or Civil affairs amongst Men, who are so inclined to Err, and apt to Change their fashions; *Nam est Natura hominum Novitatis Avida.* That for the Churches through those many Ages and in their several Communities, to agree in their Discipline amongst themselves and not Essentially to differ from those Churches that were truly Apostolical, invincibly Infers, that their Original was Divine. But this will appear more plainly when we have made and unified our *Survey.*

2. The Second Grand Division of Time, contains the space of the next Twelve hundred years, downward, more or less: within which Circuit is included the Commencement, and Progress of a Direful Apostasy, both as to Worship, and Government in the Churches. Some Symptoms of these things were rising within the former Division of time, but in this they grew a great pace, and to that decree, that the Christian World became a Notorious Apostare. For as we have it in the Idea of the Reformation, the Great Lord of time allowed a space, wearing the Denomination of Time, Times, and half a Time; of in plainer Expressions, twelve hundred and sixty years; in which space, all the Effects of a horrible Apostacy made a very *Gehennon* of that which was called Christendom. And says Dr. Ow-

en, [in his Preface, to the Inquiry, into the Original of the Churches] *Ambros* judged, that it was the Pride, or Ambition of the Doctors of the Church, which Introduced the Alternation in its Order. And moreover says the Dr. somewhat after this manner, *viz.* 'the Ambition of Church Rulers, in the fourth & fifth Centuries openly proclaimed it self to the scandal of the Christian Religion; for that their Interest lead them to a Deviation from the Order and Discipline of the Church according to its first Institution: For that the Directions given about it in Scripture, make it a matter so weighty in it self, and attended with so many Difficulties, it being laid under such severe Interdictions of Lordly power, or seeking either of Wealth or Dignity; That it's no pleasant thing to Flesh, and Blood, to engage in the conduct, and oversight of Christ's volunteers, to bear with their manners; to exercise patience towards them in all their Infirmities and in all their weaknesses, to continue a high valuation for them, as the Flock of God, which he hath purchased with his own Blood: All this requires abundance of self denial; And if so, then it's no wonder, that many of their Prelates were willing gradually to Extricate themselves out of this uneasy Condition; and embrace all Opportinities of Introducing, another Order into the Churches, that might tend more to the Exaltation of their own power and dignity. And this was done accordingly, for the Bishops by their Arbitrary Rules shared the Flock of Christ amongst themselves, and that without the consent of the People, as though they had Conquered them by the Sword. For thus they divide the spoil. This Bishop say they, shall have such a share and number of them under his power; And that Other Bishop shall have so many; And so far shall the Jurisdiction of one Extend, and so far another; that they soon Canton out the whole Roman Empire under a few Patriarchs, and head Men. These things were the subject of their Decrees and Laws, which [those of Christ's being thrown by] were now become a Rule for the Churches. But yet neither did the Bishops long keep within those Bounds and Limits, which their more modest Ambition had at first Prescribed unto them; but went on, and took Occasion from these beginnings to contend amongst themselves about Preheminency, Dignity, and Power: in which Contest, the Bishop of *Rome*, at length remained Master of the Field; And so *Rome* obtained the second Conquest of the World. And then his Holiness the head of it came to ride Admiral of all the *Sees*; and then soon became Lord of

Heaven and Earth by the same Rule of Process which brought him to his high Trust. Hence

Quaery, What can't wakeful Ambition, Learning and Fraud do, it joyntly agreed, at rifling the greatest Treasures bequeathed to Mankind; especially when the World is generally gotten into a sleepy fit?

3. Towards the latter End of this space of time began a glorious Reformation. Many famous Persons, memorable in Ecclesiastical History, being moved by the spirit of God, and according to Holy Writ, lead the way in the face at all danger; such has *Wickliff*, who openly Decryed the Pope, as the very Antichrist; in the fourteenth Century, and others in that Age. And in the next Century *Martin Luther* pursued the Reformation with great Boldness, Resolution, and Constancy. This is that famous *Luther*, says my Author, of whom they who acknowledge the least, must yet make as much as Dr. More makes of him;, for faith the Dr. I cannot think so very highly of *Luther* as some do; and yet I think him to have been a very happy, Instrument in the hand of God, for the good of Christendom against the horrid Enormities of the Papal Hyrarchy. And though he might not be allowed to be the Elias, the Conducter & Chariot of Ifracl, as some have stiled him; yet I think at least he might be accounted a faithful Postilion in that Chariot, who was well accoutred with his Wax Boots, Oiled Coat, and Hood; & who turned the Horses Noses into a direct way from *Babylon* toward the City of God, and held on in a good round Trot, through thick and thin, not caring to bespatter others in this high fogg, as he himself was finely bespattered by others; About which Time Zuinglius, Occolampadius, Melancthon and other Christian Heroes also Lifted into the same Quarrel, and with great bravery and self denial went forward with the Reformation. Yet after the endeavours of such Men, and others without number, through several Ages downward; the Churches, which are called Reformed, attained to a very imperfect Reformation, as Dr. Increase Mather says. And the defect has not been so much in Doctrine, as in Worship and Discipline. And notwithstanding, says the Dr. in this Respect also, some Churches have gone beyond others. Now to come to what I aim at; These Churches of *New-England*, as to their Order and Discipline have surpassed all Churches of the Reformation. And under the head of Discipline, if seems to me, that Christ the Captain of Salvation, has given out his Word to these

Churches, as to his Troops coming up in the Reer of Time; And his Word of Command is, — as you were; make good the Old front; or place your selves in that Regimental Order, which the Primitive Churches were in, whilst they march't under my Banners, & encountred the Devil in their heathen Persecuters for the first Three hundred years. For that the Churches in New England, and the Primitive Churches are Eminently parallel in their Government. Those first Ages of the Church it is certain were many times much annoyed with many Pestilent and Damnable Heresies; and many Usages in Worship, too Superstitious crept in amongst them; yet they continued in the Constitution of their Church Order very Uniform and Apostolical. And it is very Obvious that these Churches in this Wilderness, in the Essentials of Government; are every way Parallel to them.

I shall Represent this Business by a Collection of Parallel Notes out of several Authors of unquestionable veracity; and shall principally follow the Guidance of one who has concealed his Name; and stiles his Treatise, 'An Inquiry into the Constitution, Discipline, Unity and Worship of the Primitive Churches. This Author in his Praeface gives this fair account of his doings; says he. What I have written I have wholly Collected out of the Genuine, and Unquestionably Authentick Writings of those ages; meaning such as writ in, or of the Three first Centuries of Christianity. And says he, I have been every way Honest and Unbiast. And being well assured of his Fidelity; I shall endeavour to Imitate his Faithfulness, in Transcribing what I find in him suiting my present purpose. And I shall be well and sufficiently furnished when I have laid before the Reader the notion which the Ancients had of the Church in its Constituent parts both of Officers and People, with the several Authorities, Powers, Rights, Immunities and Prerogatives belonging unto each. And if we find that the Primitive Churches in their Order and Discipline, aid exactly agree in the Essentials of Government; with the Churches in New-England; we may Rationally then conclude that if they were Apostolical, so are we.

Chap. II. Of the Church,

To pass over all other Observations, the most usual and common Accepurion of the word *Church*, of which we must chiefly Treat, is that of a Particular Church; which consists of a Society of Christians, meeting together in one Place, under their proper Pastors, for the performance of Religious Worship, and the Exercising of Christian Discipline. This description of a Church is agreeable with the *Idiom* both of Scripture and Antiquity. Thus *Tertullian,* who Lived about the End of the Second Century, gives us an account of the State, Order & Worship of the Churches. (*Apol. ad Gen.* Cap. 39.) The Description of a Church he first lays down in these words, *viz.. Corpus fumus de Confeientia Religionis, et Disciplinae Unitate, et Spei Foedere,* We are a Body united in the Conscience of Religion, or for the Conscientious Observation of the Duties of Religion; by an Agreement in Discipline, and in a Covenant of Hope. For whereas such a Body, or Religious Society could not be United but by a Covenant; he calls it a Covenant of Hope, because the principal respect therein was had unto the things hoped for. This Religious Body, or Society thus United by Covenant, did meet together in the same Assembly, or Congregation. For says he, *Corpus sumus, Coimus in Coetum, et Congregationem ut ad Deum,* &c. We are a Body, and meet in an Assembly, and Congregation, to offer up our Prayers unto God, and attend the Duties of the Christian Religion. So Iraeneus also in the Second Century, tells us, *That some of the Brethren, and sometimes the whole Church of some certain Places— by Fasting and Prayer have Raised the Dead.* Thus our own Platform agrees in sense with the Opinion of the Ancients. Plat. Chap. 2. Sect. 6. *A Congregational Churchy is by the Institution of Christ, a part of the Militant Church., Consisting of a Company of Saints by Calling, United into one Body by an holy Covenant.,* &c. But as to the Independency, or real distinction between Church and Church; this will more clearly appear in what follows. Therefore I shall proceed to consider the Constituent Parts of a Church, as divided,

1. Into the People who Composed the Body of the Church, called the Elect, or the Called and Sanctified by the Will of God, and sometimes they are called the Brethren, because of their Brotherly Love, &c.

2. Into those Persons who were set apart for Office, or for a Peculiar and Ecclesiastical Improvement. And each Party under this distribution, had their particular Immunities and Imployments. And under these Heads, I shall confine the Discourse to a parallel in the Essentials in Government or Church Order, between the Churches of Christ in the first Ages of Christianity, and the Churches of *New-England,* as settled by their Platform.

Chap. III.

I Shall Proceed to distribute & Enumerate the Operations and Immunities of the Churches.

1. With relation to the Peculiar Acts of the Officers.

2. The Peculiar Acts of the Laity, or Fraternity.

3. The Joynt Acts of them both; as performing the Work and Bufiuefs of an Organick Church, or compleat Corporation. And

4. I shall Lastly, make some Observations upon the Union of Distinct Churches, by Acts of Sisterly Fellowship or Communion. And hereby I shall compleat the Parallel, in the Essentials of Order, between the Primitive Churches, and those of this Country.

I. The Peculiar Acts of the Officers or Clergy. Under this Head might be considered the Functions of every Particular Order, and Degree of the Clergy; which we miy say were according to the purest Antiquity, but three, *viz,.* Bishops, Priests or Presbyters, and Deacons. I shall principally consider the Bishop as the Chief Officer in Trust and Dignity, in the Primitive Church. And in order to it,

I. In general Observe, That tho' there were some Distinctions in point of a Titular Dignity and Degree, between a Bishop and Presbyter, yet they were really equal in Order, and in the Nature of their Trust. For that in an Ecclesiastical Sense, Bishop and Presbyters are Svnonimous Terms, setting forth the same Office, and signifie no more but an Elder, a Pastor, Ruler, or Overseer of a Church. *Ignatius* calls the Apostles themselves the Presbyters of the Church; and *Theodoret* renders the reason of the Appellation, for faith he, 'The Holy Scriptures called the Chief Men of Israel, the Senate, or Eldership *Wilf. Dict.* And indeed according to the Apostle himself, Presbyters, or Elders, and Bishops, are plainly Terms of Office; and of equal signification. As in Tit. I. 5, 7. *For this cause left I thee in Crete, that thou shouldest - Ordain Elders. - For a Bishop must be Blameless, as the Steward of God,* &c.

In this Discourse I shall represent the Bishop in the sense of the Primitive Churches, as Head and Chief Officer of the Church; for according to *Cyprian,* there was but one Bishop, strictly so called, in a Church at a time, tho' at the same time there were many Elders or Presbyters in the same Church; and the Bishop in a peculiar manner was Related to his Flock, as a Pastor to his Sheep and a Parent to his Children. *Cyp. Epist.* 38. § 1. *p.* 90. And the Titles of this Supream Church Officer, are most of them reckoned up in one place, in *Cyp. Epist.* 96. *viz.,* Bishop, Pastor, President, Governour, Superintendant or Priest. And this Officer is he, which in the *Revelation,* is called *The Angel of the Church,* as *Origen* thinks.

1. We may consider more distinctly, the Object of his Care, or the Dimensions of the Bishops Diocese. It's very obvious, that this Great and Superiour Officer, as has been said; had but one Church under his Pastoral Care. The Dioceses Government or Dominion of these Reverend Prelates, are never [according to Antiquity] said to contain Churches, in the Plural, but only a Church, in the Singular Number. And the Bishop was usually called the Bishop of this or that Church. As *Tertullian* faith, *Polycarp* was Ordained Bishop of the Church of *Smyrna,* &c. And moreover it is accurately to be observed, that the most frequent word used to Denominate the Extent of the Bishops Care, or to set out the Limits of his Diocese, was that of a Parish. So in the Synodical Epistle of *Irenaeus* to *Victor*, The Bishopricks of *Afia* are called Parishes: And in the History of *Eusebius*, the word is so applied in several hundred places. It's very usual there to Read of Bishops of this and that Parish. As the Bishop of the Parish in *Alexandria,* the Bishop of the Parish in *Ephesus*, and in *Corinth, &c.* For that the word *Paroikia,* which we render *Parish,* signifies *Housing,* or *Living* together. And in Ordinary and Civil life, it notes a Village, small Town, or part of a Town, of People or Persons Dwelling together. And in a Church sense it signifies a competent Number of Christians Dwelling near together, and having one Bishop, Pastor or Minister, or more, set over them; with whom they meet at one Time or Place, to Worship and Serve God. So that Parish in this sense, is the same with a Particular-Church or Congregation. And this is plainly agreeable with the Sense, Custome & Platform of *New-England* Churches.

3. That the Bishops Diocese exceeded not the Bounds of a Parish, or a small Town, or part of a Town, is very evident from the following *Demonstrations*, according to Antiquity.

Demonst. I. For that all the People of a Diocese did every *Sunday*, meet together in one Place, to Celebrate Divine Service. Thus faith *Justin Martyr*, [*Apol.* 2. p. 98.] All Assemble together in one Place, where the Bishop Preaches, and Prays.

Demonst, 2. The Bishop had but one Altar, of Communion-Table in his Diocese, at which his whole Flock Received the Sacrament from him. There is but one Alrar says *Ignatius* [*Epist ad Phila.* p. 41.] as there is but one Bishop. So says *Cyprian*, we Celebrate the Sacrament; the whole Brotherhood being present. And thus it was in *Justin Martyrs* Days. The Bishops whole Diocese met together on *Sunday*, when the Bishop gave them the Eucharist.

Demonst. 3. All the People of a Diocese were prefenr at Church Censures; as *Origen* describes an Offender, as appearing before the whole Church. In *Mat. Tom.* 13. *Pag.* 135. *Vol.* 1. So *Clemens Romanus* calls the Censures of the Church, the things Commanded by the Multitude.

Demonst. 4. No Offenders were Restored again to the Churches Peace, without the Knowledge and Consent of the whole Diocese; they were 10 plead their Cause before the whole People, &c.

Demonst. 5. When the Bishop of a Church was Dead, all the People of that Church met together in one Place to Choose a new Bishop. So *Sabinus* was chosen Bishop of *Emetria*, by the Suffrage of all the Brotherhood. The whole Diocese of the Bishops did meet together to manage Church Affairs. Thus when the Schism of *Felicissimus*, in the Bishoprick of *Carthage* was to be Debated, it was to be done according to the Will of the People, & by the Consent of the Laity. And when there were some hot Disputes about the Restitution of the Lapfed, *Cyprian* promised his whole Diocese, that all those things should be Examined before them, and judged by them. So that from the Premises, it is very evident, that the Diocese cannot possibly be more than one single Congregation; nor that Church more than a Congregational Church, where all the People and Members of that Church meet together at one time, and in one place to Pray together, to Receive the Sacrament together; Assist at Church-Censures together, and Dispatch Church Affairs together. And it is very apparent, that this was the Method and Way of the

Primitive Churches, according to the Proceeding Observation. And *New England* Churches harmonize exactly in their common Practice, as tho' they had taken their Directions from them.

4. The Bishops Duty, or the several Particular Operations of his Honourable Office, were such as these, *viz.* Preaching of the Word, Praying with his People, Administring the Sacraments, taking care of the Poor, Ordaining of Ministers, Governing his Flock, Excommunicating of Offenders, and absolving of Penitents. In a word, Whatever can be comprised under those three General Heads of Preaching, Worship, and Government, were parts of the Bishops Function and Office. And this also is very agreeable with our Platform: *Cap.* 10 *Sex.* 8. *The Power which Christ hath Committed to the Elders, is to Feed and Rule the Church of God,* &c.

Chap. IV. The Prerogatives, or Peculiar Immunities of the Laity.

THE Fraternity or Body of the People had several high Immunities Inherent in them; and Exercised by them as a Church. As,

1. Voting and giving their Suffrage, for the Admission and Censure of Members. To this purpose before.

2. The Electing their own Officers. For when a Parish, or Bishoprick was vacant through the Death of the Incumbent, the Members of that Parish met in Church to choose a fit person for his Successor, to whom they might commit the Care and Government of the Church. When *Alexander* was chosen Bishop of *Jerusalem,* [says *Eusebius, Lib.* 6. *Cap.* 11.] it was by compulsion or choice of the Members of that Church. And so in the Church of *Rome* when their Bishop was deceased; all the People met in the Church to choose a Successor. *Euseb. Lib.* 6. *Cap.* 28. Though it is certain that after some time the aspiring Clergy rob'd the People of this as well as of other of their Rights. As it is well Represented by a late very worthy Anomolous Author, writing *de Ordinatione* P. 30. *Crescente Paulatim Cleri Potestate ad fe magis indies,* &c. The Power of the Clergy gradually increasing, they daily drew more new Rights to themselves, which they took from the People; Thinking that the dignity which they had obtained, was not ample enough, if the People had

any share with them in Elections. Therefore at length snatch or take the whole Business into their own hands. The People through their supine negligence not much opposing of them. Yet that the People might be husht into quiet [with much Grace] they grant them the favour of Beggars, *viz. Postulare*; To ask for an Officer. But this plundering of the Churches falls within the Second Grand Division of Time. Not within the first three hundred years.

3. Of Approbating of Ordination. All the People were consulted and none were Admitted into holy Orders without their Approbation. As we are assured by Cyprian [*Epist.* 33.] who tells us it was his constant custom, in all Ordinations to consult his People, and with their common Counsel to weigh the Merit of every Candidate of the Sacred Orders.

4. Of Deposing of their own Officers the way. *Pag.* 96. *Sect.* 2. For if their Bishops proved Scandalous and Wicked in Life; Heretical and Apostates from the Faith, the Churches had Power to degrade and depose them, and choose others in their Room. There is a peculiar Example of this kind in a Letter from the Church of *Rome* to the Church of *Corinth,* written by *Clemens Romanus, Euseb. Lib.* 3. *Cap.* 14. upon which Dr. *Owen* makes this Observation, *viz. That the Church of Corinth was fallen into a sinful Excess in the deposition of their Elders, whom the Church of Rome judged to have presided amongst them Laudibly. ---- But yet in the whole Epistle the Church of* Corinth *is no where reproved, for assuming an Authority to themselves which did not belong to them*. It seems what Cyprian afterward affirmed, was then acknowledged, namely, *that the Right of choosing the Worthy, and Rejecting the Unworthy was in the Body of the People*. But the *Corinthian* Church is severely reproved for the abuse of their Libertie and Power, *State of Churches*, P. 94. Also when two *Spanish* Bishops were deposed by their Churches, that the said Churches might not seem to act by a Power which belonged not to them; they lent into *Africa* to several Bishops to know their judgment thereupon, who being Convened in a Synod [*Anno.* 258.] whereof *Cyprian* was President, they commended, and approved their Procedings, assuring them it was according to the Divine Law, which was Express, that none but those that were holy and blameless, should approach God's Altar; that if they had continued to have communicated with their Prophane Bishops, they would have been accessory to their Guilt and Villany, and would

24

have contradicted those Examples, and Commands in Scripture, which obliged a People to separate from Wicked, and Ungodly Ministers, that they had not acted Irregularly in what they had done; since the People had the chief Power in choosing worthy Bishops, so also of refusing those who were unworthy. And many other passages there are in that Epistle which flatly assert the People's Power of deposing scandalous Bishops. Yet where the Churches were Associated to render their action more unquestionable, they had assistance from others; but yet the Power is plainly acknowledged to be inherent in the Church. *Epist.* 68. *Apud Cyp*, §. 1. 2. 3. *p.* 200. These Premises are very Harmonious with the Constitution of these Churches. *Platf. C.* to. *Sect.* 5. 6. The Power which is granted by Christ to the Body of the Church, and Brotherhood is a Prerogative.

1. In choosing their own Officers.

2. In the Admission, and Censures of their own Members. And,

3. In case an Elder offend incorrigibly &c. as they had Power to call him to Office; so they have Power according to Order to remove him from his Office, &c.

Chap. V.

WE come nextly to consider the Joynt acts of Officers and People, carrying on, as an Organick Body. And these Peculiarly refer to the Discipline and good Government of the Church. And though Ministerial trust [precisely considered] was solely devolved on the Officers; yet still the Fraternity stood interested in, and possessed of a share in the Juridical part of Government, the whole Church in ordinary Cases were the Judges which composed the Ecclesiastical Consistory. So that the Power of the Keys was so lodged both in the Bishops and People, as that each had a share to Exercise and Improve in Joynt acts of Judicature, and thus the Clergy and Laity conjunctly made up that Supream Court which was in every Parish, where all Church Offenders were tryed, and when found Guilty, were sentenced and Condemned. That the Laity did Exercise Judicial Power in the Church, is further evident from several Testimonies. As in that of *Clemens Romanus*. [*Epist.* I. *Ad Corinth*, p 69.] where he writes: *Who will say according to the Example of* Moses. *If Seditions, Contentions, and Schisms are happened because of me, I will depart, I will go whethersoever you please, and I will do what shall be injoyned me by the People, so the Church of Christ be in Peace.* So *Origen* describes a Criminal appearing before the whole Church. In *Mar. Tom.* 13. *Cyprian,* when some had committed some great misdemeanours, professes himself not a sufficient judge, but they ought to be tryed by all the People, *Epist.* 28. p. 64, And to the same purpose, he writes of other Delinquents; *viz. That such matters should be adjusted according to the Arbitrament, and common Council of the People, and that the Lapsed in admitting them to Communion, should plead their cause before the Clergy, and before all the People.* And concerning such matters he writes to the People, *that when it would please God to restore Peace to the Church, and reduce him from Exile, then the case of the Delinquents should be examined in their Presence, and according to their Judgment.* And *Cyprian* writes in another Place, that all things were debated in common amongst them. And that whoever was Excommunicated it was by the Suffrages of the People. And though the Elders were Principally concerned, in preparing cases for the Churches Cognizance; yet its plain that the Decisive Suffrage was [in part] the Prerogative of the People. To this purpose we have an instance in some that joyned in the Schism of *Novatus;* who being sensible of their fault, came into the Presbitery, and desired the Churches Peace, the Presbytery accepted their submission, and proposed it to the whole Church, who readily embraced it. Now it is to be observed, that agreeably with the forecited Practice of the Primitive Churches, our own Platform has decided the Question concerning the Subject, and Exercise of Government;, *Platf. C.* 10. *Sect.* 11. The Ordinary Power of Government belongs only to the Elders; and Power of Priviledge remaineth with the Brotherhood, [as the Power of Judgment in matters of Censure, and Power of Liberty in matters of Liberty] thence it follows, that in an Organick Church, and Right Administration, all Church acts proceed after the manner of a mixt Administration, so that no Church act can be consummated, or perfected without the consent of both.

Chap. VI.

4. I Shall nextly consider the Fellowship and Communion that Distinct Churches had & held one with another.

It is very obvious by this Time, [and he must blind his own Eyes that won't see it] That the Primitive Churches [according to the Account we have of their Regiment for the first three hundred years from Christ] were distinct Political Bodies; and neither Diocesan, Rational, Provincial nor Classical, but properly Congregational Churches. And as such, were perfect and compleat Societies Incorporate, so that they had a Power, and Capacity of carrying on all Church-work within themselves, and wanted not to borrow, or receive from others, for the support of their Being, and so were Independent. Yet considering they were imperfect in their Matter, and therefore to help forward their Well-being, wanted the advantage of all good means, with the influence of the Grace, Love, Knowledge, Experience, Wisdom, and Counsel of each other; so they were dependent, and became mutually Officious, and accountable each to other: Somewhat after the manner, as Mr. *Hooker* distinguishes on the Independency, and Dependency of Gospel Churches. *Pol. Lib.* 2. *Chap* 3. Says he, *Independency implies two things.* Either,

1. *An absolute Supremacy, opposed to Subordination, and so a Particular Church is not Independent, it being accountable to Civil Government, &c. and also to the Consociation of Churches.* Or,

2. *Independency signifies a sufficiency in its kind, for the attainment of its End. And in this sense, Independency is opposed to Imperfection: And if we take it thus, then a Particular Church may be said to be Independent, it being sufficient to attain the end it was Instituted for; it having compleat powers when rightly Constituted, to Exercise all the Ordinances of God. And thus we find, that the Primitive Churches in this sense were Independent Churches: That is, every Particular Church had a sufficient Right and Power, without the Concurrence and Authority of any other Church, to carry on the Worship of God, and Exercise of Discipline in their distinct Society. And yet as they were Parts of the Universal Church, held themselves obliged to a suitable Communion. And for the support of Unity, Love, and Concord amongst them, and to advise about their common Circumstances and Condition, and also to Regulate their Ecclesiastical Affairs within*

their general Limits, for their mutual advantage; did therefore form, themselves into Synodical Assemblies, and were governed in common by them; for that their Synodical Decrees, Canons or Institutions were accounted Obligatory to all the Churches, who had their Representatives in the Synods. For indeed to what purpose else did they draw up their Resolves, but for the good and benefit of the whole Community. And it would have been very fruitless to have made wearisome Journeys, with great cosh and pains to determine such things, as they judged expedient for the Churches Well-being; if after all, it were indifferent whether they were obeyed or no: Or that when the whole was agreed, some should reluct, & remonstrate; & especially when things were fairly settled by a joynt Suffrage in Synods, some small sett of Wise Men should hold themselves wiser than whole Synods; and afterward should of their own heads in their wore private Apartments set forward new Schemes, which in it self is disorderly, and a way to keep the Churches constantly fluctuating, and restless, like the unstable Ocean. And indeed, considering the Regularity, Wisdom and Union in Synodical Settlements, whilst that all sorts of persons interested, both Officers and People having had their full liberty in Debates, and their free Votes and Suffrages, in drawing up the Decrees and Settlements; it is a bold intrusion, and little better than defying and trampling under foot the Unity, Love, Honour and Authority of the Churches, to run counter with Synodical Settlements, till they are fairly Repealed by the like Power which made the Settlements. And thus we come to consider the Members of the Synods of the Primitive Churches.

And these were Bishops, Presbyters, Deacons, and Deputed Lay men, in behalf of the People of their Respective Churches. At a great Synod at *Antioch,* which condemned *Paulus Samosatenus,* there were present Bishops, Presbyters, Deacons, and the Church of God; that is Laymen, who represented the People of their several Churches. *Euseb.* l. 7 *Cap.* 30. Also when the Heresie of the *Montanists,* was fixed and preached, the Faithful in *Asia* met together several times to Examine it, and upon Examination condemned it. *Euseb. lib.* 5. *Cap.* 16. Also there being some heats in the Church of *Carthage,* about the Restitution of the Lapsed, *Cyprian,* Bishop of that Church, writes from Exile, *That there should be Convened a Synod of Bishops, and of the Laity, who had stood firm thro' the Persecution, to Consult about, and Determine their Affairs.* Epist. 14. And moreover

28

at a great Synod held at *Carthage, Anno* 258. there were present Eighty Seven Bishops, together with Presbyters and Deacons, and a great part of the Laity. *Apud Cypri, p.* 443.

The Principles of the Churches in New-*England,* Asserting the Right of the People in Synodal Meetings, is fully set down in the Chapter concerning Synods. *Platf.* And the Practice of these in Harmony with the Primitive Churches has been all along agreeable to it. In the last Synod which was in New-England, in the year 1679. Some Churches sent only their Elders without their Brethren, with which the Synod was so far unsatisfyed, as that they would not allow those Pastors to Sit with them, until they had prevailed with their Churches to send Brethren also; being very tender of Admitting any thing, that should look like the Infringement of that Liberty and Priviledge, which does by the Institution of Christ belong to the Brotherhood in Particular Churches. Dr. *Mathers Order. Q.* 11. I shall conclude this Head or Demonstration with these Weighty and Solemn Words of the Learned and Famous Mr. *Oakes,* Praesident of the Colledge, in his Election Sermon. *Consider* (says he) *what will he the End of Receding, or making of a Defection from the way of Church Government established amongst us. I profess that I look upon the Discovery and Settlement of the Congregational Way as the Boon, the Gratuity, the largess of Divine Bounty, which the Lord graciously bestowed on this People, that followed him into this Wilderness, and who were separated from their Brethren. Those Good People who came over had more Love, Zeal, and affectionate desire of Communion with God, in pure Worship and Ordinances, and did more in order to it, than others; and the Lord did more for them than for any People in the World, in shewing them the Pattern of his House, and the truer Scriptural-way of Church-Government and Administrations, God was certainly in a more than ordinary way present with his Servants, in laying of our Foundations; and in settling Church-Order, according to the Will and Appointment of Christ. Consider what will be the sad issue of Revolting from the way fixed on to one extream or to another, whether it he to Presbyterianism or Brownism.* 'As for the Presbyterians, it must be acknowledged, that there are amongst them, as Pious, Learned, Sober, Orthodox Men, as the World affords, and that there is as much of the Power of Godliness among that Party, and of the Spirit of the good old Puritans, as among any People in the World. And as for the Ways of their Church Government, it must be confessed, that in the day of it, it was a very considerable step to Reformation. The Reformation in King *Edward's* Days, was a blessed work; and the Reformation of *Geneva* and *Scotland,* was then a larger step, and in many respects purer than the other. And for my part, I fully believe that the Congregational-way far exceeds both, and is the highest step that has been taken towards Reformation, and for the substance of it, it is the very same way that was Established and Practised in the Primitive Times, according to the Institution of Jesus Christ. Thus ends my first Demonstration in a fair parallel drawn up between the Holiest Churches that ever were in the World, and the Churches of New-England; and however they may differ in their Morals, they are very harmonious in their Order. And considering that the former cannot rationally be thought but they derived their Constitution from the Apostles, and so it must needs be of a Divine Original: And if so, then these in *New-England* who are fashioned so exactly like them, must needs be of the same Pedigree, *&c.* But I shall wave all Improvement of the Premises, and leave the whole to the serious and judicious thoughts of every Impartial Reader, not doubting but he will find sufficient evidence of the Divine Original of these Churches in what has been said. And that I might now obtain a *Supersedeas*, and forbear adding any further Plea in their Defence. But yet to gratifie my own Curiosity, and divert the Reader, I shall proceed to Inquire into the Natural Reason of the Constitution of those Churches we have been comparing, la this Question I shall go out of the Common Road, and take into an unusual and unbeaten Path; wherein possibly I may fall into some Thickets now and then, and be somewhat intangled, yet I hope the Candid Reader will afford some succour by his tender Clemency, and his friendly Interpretation of my good Intentions. For tho' I may in so devious a way, miss of some part of the Truth; yet I have a great presumption that I may open a Road to Men of greater Learning, and a deeper Search, that will lead to a rich Treasure of Knowledge, and Wisdom, for Ease and Relief under those many Questions and crabbed Debates concerning Church-Government in the Christian World; for to me it seems most apparent, that under Christ the reason of the Constitution of these and the primitive Churches, is really and truly owing to the Original State and Liberty of Mankind, and founded peculiarly in the Light of Nature. And thus I come to the

2. Demonstration in Defence of our *Platform,* which is founded in the Light of Nature.

Chap. I

THE Divine Establishment in Providence of the fore-named Churches in their Order is apparently the Royal assent of the supream Monarch of the Churches, to the grave Decisions of Reason in favour of Man's Natural state of Being, and Original Freedom. For it we should make a new *Survey* of the Constitution before named under the brightest Light of Nature, there is no greater Example of natural Wisdom in any settlement on Earth; for the present and future security of Humane Beings in all that is most Valuable and Grand, then in this. That it seems to me as though Wise and Provident Nature by the Dictates of Right Reason excited by the moving Suggestions of Humanity; and awed with the just demands of Natural Libertie, Equity, Equality, and Principles of Self-Preservation, Originally drew up the Scheme, and then obtained the Royal Approbation. And certainly it is agreeable that we attribute it to God whether we receive it nextly from Reason or Revelation, for that each is equally an Emanation of his Wisdom, *Prov.* 20. 27. The Spirit of Man is the Candle of the Lord, searching all the inward parts of the Belly. There be many larger Volumns in this dark Recess called the Belly to be read by that Candle God has Light up. And I am very well assured the forenamed Constitution is a transcript out of some of their Pages, Joh. 1. 4, 9. *And the Life was the Light of Men, which Lighteth every Man which cometh into the World.* This admirable Effect of Christs Creating Power in hanging out so many Lights to guide man through a dark World, is as Applicable to the Light of Reason, as to that of Revelation. For that the Light of Reason as a Law and Rule of Right, is an Effect of Christ's goodness, care and creating Power, as well as of Revelation; though Revelation Natures Law in a fairer and brighter Edition. This is granted by the *London* Ministers, *P.* 8. *C.* 3. 'That, that which is evident by, and consonant to the true Light of Nature, or Natural Reason, is to be accounted, *Jure Divino,* in matters of Religion. But in the further and more distinct management of this Plea; I shall,

1. Lay before the Reader several Principles Natural Knowledge.

2. Apply or Improve them in Ecclesiastical affairs.

3. Inferr from the Premises, a Demonstration that these Churches, if not properly Formed; yet are fairly Established in their present Order by the Law of Nature.

Chap II.

I. I Shall disclose several Principles of Natural Knowledge; plainly discovering the Law of Nature; or the true sentiments of Natural Reason, with Respect to Man's Being and Government. And in this Essay I shall peculiarly confine the discourse to two heads, *viz.*

1. Of the Natural [in distinction to the Civil] and then,

2. Of the Civil Being of Man. And I shall Principally take Baron *Puffendorff* for my Chief Guide and Spokesman.

1. I shall consider Man in a state of Natural Being, as a Free-Born Subject under the Crown of Heaven, and owing Homage to none but God himself. It is certain Civil Government in General, is a very Admirable Result of Providence, and an Incomparable Benefit to Mankind, yet must needs be acknowledged to be the Effect of Humane Free-Compacts and not of Divine Institution; it is the Produce of Man's Reason, of Humane and Rational Combinations, and not from any direct Orders of Infinite Wisdom, in any positive Law wherein is drawn up this or that Scheme of Civil Government. Government [says the Lord *Warrington*] is necessary — in that no Society of Men can subsist without it; and that Particular Form of Government is necessary which best suits the Temper and Inclination of a People. Nothing can be God's Ordinance, but what he has particularly Declared to be such; there is no particular Form of Civil Government described in God's Word, neither does Nature prompt it. The Government of the *Jews* was changed five Times. Government is not formed by Nature, as other Births or Productions; If it were, it would be the same in all Countries; because Nature keeps the same Method, in the same thing, in all Climates. If a Common Wealth be changed into a Monarchy, is it Nature that forms, and brings forth the Monarch? Or if a Royal Family wholly Extinct [as in *Noah's* Case, being not Heir Apparent from Descent from *Adam*] is it Nature that must go to work [with the King Bees, who themselves

alone preserve the Royal Race in that Empire] to Breed a Monarch before the People can have a King, or a Government sent over them? And thus we must leave Kings to Resolve which is their best Title to their Crowns, whether Natural Right, or the Constitution of Government settled by Humane Compacts, under the Direction and Conduct of Reason. But to proceed under the head of a State of Natural Being, I shall more distinctly Explain the State of Humane Nature in its Original Capacity, as Man is placed on Earth by his Maker, and Cloathed with many Investitures, and Immunities which properly belong to Man separately considered. As,

1. The Prime Immunity in Man's State, is that he is most properly the Subject of the Law of Nature. He is the Favourite Animal on Earth; in that this Part of Gods Image, *viz*. Reason is Congenate with his Nature, wherein by a Law Immutable, Instampt upon his Frame, God has provided a Rule for Men in all their Actions, obliging each one to the performance of that which is Right, not only as to Justice, but likewise as to all other Moral Vertues, the which is nothing but the Dictate of Right Reason founded in the Soul of Man. *Molloy, De Mao, Praef.* That which is to be drawn from Mans Reason, flowing from the true Current of that Faculty, when unperverted, may be said to be the Law of Nature; on which account, the Holy Scriptures declare it written on Mens hearts. For being indowed with a Soul, you may know from your self, how, and what you ought to act, *Rom.* 2. 14. *These having not a Law, are a Law in themselves.* So that the meaning is, when we acknowledge the Law of Nature to be the dictate of Right Reason, we must mean that the Understanding of Man is Endowed with such a power, as to be able, from the Contemplation of humane Condition to discover a necessity of Living agreeably with this Law: And likewise to find out some Principle, by which the Precepts of it, may be clearly and solidly Demonstrated. The way to discover the Law of Nature in our own state, is by a narrow Watch, and accurate Contemplation of our Natural Condition, and propensions. Others say this is the way to find out the Law of Nature. *foil.* If a Man any ways doubts, whether what he is going to do to another Man be agreeable to the Law of Nature, then let him. suppose himself to be in that other Mans Room; And by this Rule effectually Executed. A Man must be a very dull Scholar to Nature not to make Proficiency in the Knowledge of her Laws. But more

Particularly in pursuing our Condition for the discovery of the Law of Nature, this is very obvious to view, *viz.*

1. A Principle of Self-Love, & Self-Preservation, is very predominant in every Mans Being.

2. A Sociable Disposition.

3. An Affection or Love to Mankind in General. And to give such Sentiments the force of a Law, we must suppose a God who takes care of all Mankind, and has thus obliged each one, as a Subject of higher Principles of Being, then meer Instincts. For that all Law properly considered, supposes a capable Subject, and a Superiour Power; And the Law of God which is Binding, is published by the Dictates of Right Reason as other ways: Therefore lays Plutarch, *To follow God and obey Reason is the same thing.* But moreover that God has Established the Law of Nature, as the General Rule of Government, is further Illustrable from the many Sanctions in Providence, and from the Peace and Guilt of Conscience in them that either obey, or violate the Law of Nature. But moreover, the foundation of the Law of Nature with relation to Government, may be thus Discovered. *foil.* Man is a Creature extreamly desirous of his own Preservation; of himself he is plainly Exposed to many wants, unable to secure his own safety, and Maintenance without the Assistance of his fellows: and he is also able of returning Kindness by the furtherance of mutual Good. But yet Man is often found to be Malicious, Insolent, and easily Provoked, and as powerful in Effecting mischief, as he is ready in designing it. Now that such a Creature may be Preserved, it is necessary that he be Sociable; that is, that he be capable and disposed to unite himself to those of his own species, and to Regulate himself towards them, that they may have no fair Reason to do him harm; but rather incline to promote his Interests and secure his Rights, and Concerns. This then is a Fundamental Law of Nature, that every Man as far as in him lies, do maintain a Sociableness with others, agreeable; with the main end and disposition of humane Nature in general. For this is very apparent, that Reason and Society render Man the most potent of all Creatures. And Finally, from the Principles of Sociableness it follows as a fundamental Law of Nature, that Man is not so Wedded to his own interest, but that he can make the Common good the mark of his Aim: And hence he becomes Capacitated to enter into a Civil State by the Law of Nature; for without this property in Nature, *viz.*

Sociableness, which is for Cementing of parts, every Government would soon moulder and dissolve.

2. The Second Great Immunity of Man is an Original Liberty Instampt upon ins Rational Nature. He that intrudes upon this Liberty, Violates the Law of Nature, in this Discourse I will wave the Consideration of Man's Moral Turpitude, but shall view him Physically as a Creature which God has made and furnished efficiently with many Enobling Immunities, which render him the most August Animal in the World, and still, whatever has happened since his Creation, he remains at the upper end of Nature, and as such is a Creature of a very Noble Character. For as to his Dominion, the whole frame of the Lower Part of the Universe is devoted, to his use, and at his Command; and his Liberty under the Conduct of Right Reason, is equal with his trust. Which Liberty may be briefly Considered, Internally as to his Mind, and Externally as to his Person.

1. The Internal Native Liberty of Man's Nature in general implies, a faculty of Doing or Omitting things according to the Direction of his Judgment. But in a more special meaning, this Liberty does not consist in a loose and ungovernable Freedom, or in an unbounded Licence of Acting. Such Licence is disagreeing with the condition and dignity of Man, and would make Man of a lower and meaner Constitution then Bruit Creatures; who in all their Liberties are kept under a better and more Rational Government, by their Instincts. Therefore as Plutarch says, Those Persons only who live in Obedience to Reason, are worthy to be accounted free: They alone live as they Will, who have Learnt what they ought to Will. So that the true Natural Liberty of Man, such as really and truely agrees to him, must be understood, as he is Guided and Restrained by the Tyes of Reason, and Laws of Nature; all the rest is Brutal, if not worse.

2. Man's External Personal, Natural Liberty Antecedent to all Humane parts, or Alliances must also be considered. And so every Man must be conceived to be perfectly in his own Power and disposal, and not to be controuled by the Authority of any other. And thus every Man, must be acknowledged equal to every Man, since all Subjection and all Command are equally banished on both sides; and considering all Men thus at Liberty, every Man has a Preroga-

tive to Judge for himself. *viz.* What shall be most for his Behoof, Happiness and Well-being.

3. the Third Capital Immunity belonging to Man's Nature, is an equality amongst Men; Which is not to be denied by the Law of Nature, till Man has Refined himself with all his Rights for the sake of a Civil State; and then his Personal Liberty and Equality is to be cherished, and preserved to the highest degree, as will consist with all just distinctions amongst Men of Honour, and shall be agreeable with the publick Good. For Man his a high valuation of himself, and the passion seems to lay its first foundation [not in Pride, but] really in the high and admirable Frame and Constitution of Humane Nature. The Word Man, says my Author, is thought to carry to somewhat of Dignity in its sound; and we commonly make use of this as the most proper and prevailing Argument against a rude Insulter, *viz. I am not a Beast or a Dog, but am a Man as well as your self.* Since then Humane Nature agrees equally with all persons; and since no one can live a Sociable Life with another that does not own or Respect him as a Man; It follows as a Command of the Law of Nature, that every Man Esteem and treat another as one who is naturally his equal, or who is a Man as well as he. There be many popular, or plausible Reasons that greatly Illustrate this Equality, *viz.* that we all Derive our Being from one stock, the same Common Father of humane Race. On this Consideration *Boethius* checks the pride of the Insulting Nobility.

Quid Genus et Proavos Strepitis?
Si Primordia Vestra,
Auteremque 'Deum Spectas,
Nullus Degener Extat
Nisi vitiis Pepora sovens,
Proprium Deserat Ortum.

Fondly our first Descent we Boast;
It whence at first our Breath we Drew,
The common Springs of Life we view,
The Airy Notion soon is Lost.

The Almighty made us equal all;
But he that slavishly complies

To do the 'Drudgery of Vice,
Denyes his high Original.

And also that our Bodies are Composed of matter, frail, brittle, and lyable to be destroyed by thousand Accidents; we all owe our Existence to the same Method of propagation. The Noblest Mortal in his Entrance on to the Stage of Life, is not distinguished by any pomp or of passage from the lowest of Mankind; and our Life hastens Co the same General Mark: Death observes no Ceremony, but Knocks as loud at the Barriers of the Court, as at the Door of the Cottage. This Equality being admitted, bears a very great force in maintaining Peace and Friendship amongst Men. For that he who would use the Assistance of others, in promoting his own Advantage, ought as freely to be at their service, when they want his help on the like Occasions. *One good turn requires another,* is the Common Proverb, for otherwise he must need esteem others unequal to himself, who constantly demands their Aid, told as constantly denies his own. And whoever is of this Insolent Temper, cannot but highly displease those about him, and soon give Occasion of the Breach of the Common Peace. It was a Manly Reproof which *Charactacus* gave the *Romans, Num Si vos Omnibus* &c. What! because you desire to be Masters of all Men, does it follow therefore that all Men should desire to be your Slaves, for that it is a Command of Nature's Law, that no Man that has not obtained a particular and special Right, shall arrogate to himself a Larger share then his fellows, but shall admit others to equal Priviledges with himself. So that the Principle of Equality in a Natural State, is peculiarly transgressed by Pride, which is when a Man without sufficient reason prefers himself to others. And though as *Henfius,* Paraphrases upon *Aristotle's* Politicks to this Purpose. *viz. Nothing is more suitable to Nature, then that those who Excel in Understanding and Prudence, should Rule and Controul those who an less happy in those advantages,* &c. Yet we must note, that there is room for an Answer, *foil.* That it would be the greatest absurdity to believe, that Nature actually Invests the Wise with a Sovereignty over the weak; or with a Right of forcing them against their Wills; for that no Sovereignty can be Established, unless some Humane Deed, or Covenant Precede: Nor does Natural fitness for Government make a Man presently Governour over another; for that as *Ulpian* says, *by a*

Natural Right all Men are born free; and Nature having set all Men upon a Level and made them Equals, no Servitude or Subjection can be conceived without Inequality; and this cannot be made without Usurpation or Force in others? or Voluntary Compliance in those who Resign their freedom, and give away their degree of Natural Being. And thus we come,

2. To consider Man in a Civil State of Being; wherein we shall observe the great difference between a Natural, and Political State; for in the Latter State many Great disproportions appear, or at least many obvious distinctions are soon made amongst Men; which Doctrine is to be laid open under a few heads.

1. Every Man considered in a Natural State, must be allowed to be Free, and at his own dispose; yet to suit Man's Inclinations to Society; And in a peculiar manner to gratify the necessity he is in of publick Rule and Order, he is Impelled to enter into a Civil Community; and Divests himself of his Natural Freedom, and puts himself under Government; which amongst other things Comprehends the Power of Life and Death over Him; together with Authority to Injoyn him some things to which he has an utter Aversation, and to prohibit him other things, for which he may have as strong an Inclination; so that he may be often under this Authority, obliged to Sacrifice his Private, for the Publick Good. So that though Man is inclined to Society, yet he is driven to a Combination by great necessity. For that the true and leading Cause of forming Governments, and yielding up Natural Liberty, and throwing Mans Equality into a Common Pile to be new Cast by the Rules of fellowship; was really and truly to guard themselves against the Injuries Men wen lyable to Interchangeably; for none so Good to Man, as Man, and yet none a greater Enemy. So that,

2. The first Humane Subject and Original of Civil Power is the People. For as they have a Power every Man over himself in a Natural State, so upon a Combination they can and do bequeath this Power unto others; and settle it according as their united discretion shall Determine. For that this is very plain, that when the Subject of Sovereign Power is quite Extinct, that Power returns to the People again. And when they are free, they may set up what species of Government they please; or if they rather incline to it, they may subside into a State of Natural Being, if it be plainly for the best. In the *Eastern* Country of the *Mogul*, we hive some resemblance of the

Case; for upon the Death of an absolute Monarch, they live so many days without a Civil Head; but in that *Interregnum,* those who survive the Vacancy, are glad to get into a Civil State again, and usually they are in a very Bloody Condition when they return under the Covert of a new Monarch; this project is to indear the People to a Tyranny, from the Experience they have so lately had of an Anarchy.

3. The formal Reason of Government is the Will of a Community, yielded up and surrendered to some other Subject, either of one particular Person, or more, Conveyed in the following manner.

Let us conceive in our Mind a multitude of Men, all Naturally Free & Equal; going about voluntarily, to Erect themselves into a new Common-Wealth. Now their Condition being such, to bring themselves into a Politick Body, they must needs Enter into divers Covenants.

1. They must Interchangeably each Man Covenant to joyn in one lasting Society, that they may be capable to concert the measures of their safety, by a Publick Vote.

2. A Vote or Decree must then nextly pass to set up some Particular species of Government over them. And if they are joyned in their first Compact upon absolute Terms to stand to the Decision of the first Vote concerning the Species of Government: Then all are bound by the Majority to acquiesce in that particular Form thereby settled, though their own private Opinion, incline them to some other Model.

3. After a Decree has specified the Particular form of Government, then there will be need of a New Covenant, whereby those on whom Sovereignty is conferred, engage to take care of the Common Peace, and Welfare, And the Subjects on the other hand, to yield them faithful Obedience. In which Covenant is Included that Submission and Union of Wills, by which a State may be conceived to be but one Person. So that the most proper Definition of a Civil State, is this. *viz.* A Civil State is a Compound Moral Person. whose Will [United by those Covenants before passed] is the Will of all; to the end it may Use, and Apply the strength and riches of Private Persons towards maintaining the Common Peace, Security, and Wellbeing of all. Which may be conceived as tho' the whole State Was now become but one Man; in which the aforesaid Covenants may be supposed under Gods Providence, to be the Divine *Fiat,*

Pronounced by God, let us make Man. And by way of resemblance the aforesaid Being may be thus Anatomized.

1. The Sovereign Power is the Soul infused, giving Life and Motion to the whole Body.

2. Subordinate Officers are the Joynts by which the Body moves.

3. Wealth and Riches are the Strength,

4. Equity and Laws are the Reason.

5. Councellors the Memory.

6. *Salus Populi,* or the Happiness of the People, is the End of its Being; or main Business to be attended and done.

7. Concord amongst the Members, and all Estates, is the Health.

8. Sedition is Sickness, and Civil War Death.

4. The Parts of Sovereignty may be considered: So,

1. As it Prescribes the Rule of Action: It Is rightly termed *Legislative Power.*

2. As it determines the Controversies of Subjects by the Standard of those Rules. So is it justly Termed Judiciary Power.

3. As it Arms the Subjects against Foreigners, or forbids Hostility, so it's called the Power of Peace and War.

4. As it takes in Ministers for the discharge of Business, so it is called the Right of Appointing Magistrates, So that all great Officers and Publick Servants, must needs owe their Original to the Creating Power of Sovereignty. So that those whose Right it is to Create, may Dissolve the being of those who are Created, unless they cast them into an Immortal Frame. And yet must needs be dissoluble if they justly forfeit their being to their Creators.

5. The Chief End of Civil Communities, is, that Men thus conjoyned, may be secured against the Injuries, they are lyable to from their own Kind. For if every Man could secure himself singly; It would be great folly for him, to Renounce his Natural Liberty, in which every Man is his own King and Protector.

6. The Sovereign Authority besides that it inheres in every State as in a Common and General Subject. So farther according as it resides in some One Person, or in a Council [consisting of some Select Persons, or of all the Members of a Community] as in a proper and particular Subject, so it produceth different Forms of Commonwealths, *viz.* Such as are either simple and regular, or mixt.

1. The Forms of a Regular State are three only, which Forms arise from the proper and particular Subject, in which the Supream Power Resides. As,

1. A Democracy, which is when the Sovereign Power is Lodged in a Council consisting of all the Members, and where every Member has the Privilege of a Vote. This Form of Government, appears in the greatest part of the World to have been the most Ancient. For that Reason seems to shew it to be most probable, that when Men [being Originally in a condition of Natural Freedom and Equality] had thoughts of joyning in a Civil Body, would without question be inclined to Administer their common Affairs, by their common Judgment and so must necessarily to gratifie that Inclination establish a Democracy; neither can it be rationally imagined, that Fathers of Families being yet Free and Independent, should in a moment, or little time take off their long delight in governing their own Affairs, & Devolve all upon some single Sovereign Commander; for that it seems to have been thought more Equitable, that what belonged to all, should be managed by all, when all had entered by Compact into one Community. The Original of our Government, says *Plato*, [speaking of the Athenian Common-Wealth] *was taken from the Equality of our Race. Other States there are composed of different Blood, and of unequal Lines, the Consequence of which are disproportionable Sovereignty, Tyrannical or Oligarchycal Sroay; under which men live in such a manner, as to Esteem themselves partly Lords, and partly Slaves to each other. But we and our Country men, being all Born Brethren of the same Mother, do not look upon ourselves, to stand under so hard a Relation, as that of Lord and Slaves; but the Parity of our Descent incline us to keep up the like Parity by our Laws, and to yield the precedency to nothing but to Superiour Vertue and Wisdom.* And moreover it seems very manifest that most Civil Communities arose at first from the Union of Families, that were nearly allyed in Race and Blood. And though Ancient Story make frequent mention of Kings, yet it appears that most of them were such that had an Influence rather in persuading, then in any Power of Commanding. So *Justin* describes that Kind of Government, as the most Primitive, which Aristotle styles an Heroical Kingdom. *viz..* Such as is no ways Inconsistent with a Democratical State. *De Princap. Reru.* 1. *L.* I. *C.*

A democracy is then Erected, when a Number of Free Persons, do Assemble together in Order to enter into a Covenant for Uniting themselves in n Body; And such a Preparative Assembly hath some appearance already of a Democracy; it is a Democracy in *Embrio*] properly in this Respect, that every Man hath the Priviledge freely to deliver his Opinion concerning the Common Affairs. Yet he who dissents from the Vote of the Majority, is not in the least obliged by what they determine, till by a second Covenant, a Popular Form be actually Established; for not before then can we call it a Democratical Government, *viz*. Till the Right of Determining all matters relating to the publick Safety, is actually placed in a General Assembly of the whole People; or by their own Compact and Mutual Agreement, Determine themselves the proper Subject for the Exercise of Sovereign Power. And to compleat this State, and render it capable to Exert its Power to answer the End of a Civil State: these Conditions are necessary.

1. That a certain Time and Place be Assigned for Assembling.

2. That when the Assembly be Orderly met, as to Time and Place, that then the Vote of the Majority must pass for the Vote of the whole Body.

3. That Magistrates be appointed to Exercise the Authority of the whole for the better dispatch of Business, of every days Occurrence; who also may with more Mature diligence, search into more Important Affairs; and if in case any thing happens of greater Consequence, may report it to the Assembly; and be peculiarly Serviceable in putting all Publick Decrees into Execution. Because a large Body of People is almost useless in Respect of the last Service, and of many others, as to the more Particular Application and Exercise of Power, Therefore it is most agreeable with the Law of Nature, that they Institute their Officers to aft in their Name, and Stead.

2. The Second Species of Regular Government,; an Aristocracy; and this is said then to be Constituted when the People, or Assembly United by a first Covenant, and having thereby cast themselves into the first Rudiments of a State; do then by Common Decree, Devolve the Sovereign Power, on a Council consisting of some Select Members; and these having accepted of the Designation, are then properly invested with Sovereign Command; and then an Aristocracy is formed.

3. The Third Species of a Regulur Government, is a Monarchy which is settled when the Sovereign Power is conferred on some one worthy Person. It differs from the former, because a Monarch who is but one Person in Natural, as well as in Moral account, & so is furnished with an Immediate Power of Exercising Sovereign Command in all Instances of Government; but the forenamed must needs have Particular Time and Place assigned, but the Power and Authority is Equal in each.

2. Mixt Governments, which are various and of divers kinds [not now to be Enumerated] yet possibly the fairest in the World is that which Has a Regular Monarchy; [in Distinction to what is Dispotick] settled upon a Noble Democracy as its Basis. And each part of the Government is so adjusted by Pacts and Laws that renders the whole Constitution an Elysium. It is said of the *British* Empire, *That it is such a Monarchy, as that by the necessary subordinate Concurrence of the Lords and Commons, in the Making and Repealing all Statutes or Acts of Parliament; it hath the main Advantages of an Aristocracy, and of a Democracy, yet free from the Disadvantages and Evils of either. It is such a Monarchy, as by most Admirable Temperament affords very much to the Industry, Liberty and Happiness of the Subject and reserves enough for the Majesty and Prerogative of any King, who will own his People as Subjects, not as Slaves. It is a Kingdom, that of all the Kingdoms of the World, is most like to the Kingdom of Jesus Christ whose Yoke is easie, and Burden light.* Present State of *England* ist Part 64 *p* Thus having drawn up this brief Scheme concerning Man, and the Nature of Civil Government, he is become sole Subject of. I shall nextly proceed to make Improvements of the Premises, to accommodate the main Subject under our Consideration.

2. I shall now make some Improvement of the foregoing Principles of Civil Knowledge, fairly deduced from the Law of Nature. And I will peculiarly refer to Ecclesiastical Affairs, whereby we may in probability discover move clearly the Kind, and something of the Nature of that Government, which Christ has plac't in and over, his Church. The Learned Debates of Men, and Divine Writ sometimes seems to cast such a Grandure on the Church & its Officers, as tho' they stood in Peerage with Civil Empire. *Rev.* 1. 6. 9. 1 *Pet.* 2. 9. 1 *Cor.* 4. 8. 1 *Cor.* 12. 28. 2 *Cor.* 10. 8. But all such Expressions must needs be other-ways Interpreted. God is the highest Cause that acts

by Council; and it must needs be altogether repugnant, to think he should fore-cast the State of this World by no better a Scheme, than to Order two Sovereign Powers, in the same Grand Community, which would be like placing two Suns in the Firmament, which would be to set the Universe into a Flame: That should such an Error happen, one must needs be forth with Extinguished, to bring the Frame of Nature into a just Temper, and keep it out of harm's way. But to proceed with my Purpose, I shall go back upon the Civil Scheme, and inquire after two things: first of Rebellion against Government in general, and then in special; whether any of the aforesaid Species of Regular Government can be predicable of the Church of God on Earth.

1. In General concerning Rebellion against Government for Particular Subjects to break in upon Regular Communities duly Established is upon the premises to Violate the Law of Nature; and is a high Usurpation upon the first grand Immunities of Mankind. Such Rebels in States, and Usurpers in Churches affront the World, with a presumption that the Best of the Brotherhood are a Company of Fools, and that themselves have fairly Monopolized all the Reason of Humane Nature. Yea, they take upon them the Boldness to assume a Prerogative of trampling under foot the natural original Equality & Liberty of their Fellows, for to push the Proprietors of Settlements out of possession of their old, and impose new Schemes upon them, is vertually to declare them in a state of Vassalage, or that they were Born so, and therefore will the Usurper be so gracious is to insure them they shall not be Sold at the next Market: They must esteem it a favour, for by this time all the Original Prerogatives of Man's Nature are intentionally a Victim, smoaking to satiate the Usurper's Ambition. It is a very tart Observation on an *English* Monarch, and where it may by proportion be applied to a Subject must needs sink very deep, and serve for evidence under this Head. It is in the Secret History of K. *C.* 2. and K *J.* 2. *p.* 2. Says my Author, *Where the Constitution of a Nation is such, that the Laws of the Land are the Measures both of the Sovereigns Commands, and the Obedience of the Subjects, whereby it is Provided; that as the one are not to Invade what by Concessions and Stipulations is granted to the Ruler; so the other is not to deprive them of their lawful and determined Rights and Liberties; then the Prince who strives to subvert the Fundamental Laws of the Society, is the Traytor and the Rebel,*

44

and not the People, who endeavour to Preserve and Defend their own. It's very applicable to particular Men in their Rebellions or Usurpations in Church of State.

2. In special I shall now proceed to Enquire, Whether any of the aforesaid Species of regular, unmixt Governments, can with any good shew of Reason be predicable of the Church of Christ on Earth. If the Churches of Christ, as Churches, are either the Object or Subject of a Sovereign Power intrusted in the hands of Men, then most certainly one of the fore-cited Schemes of perfect Government will be applicable to it.

Before I pursue the Enquiry, it may not be improper to pause, & make some Caution here, by distinguishing between that which may have some Resemblance of Civil Power, and the thing it self; and so the Power of Churches is but a faint Resemblance of Civil Power; it comes in reality nothing near to the thing it self; for the one is truly Coercive, the other persuasive; the one is Sovereign Power, the other is Delegated and Ministerial. But not to delay, I shall proceed with my Enquiry, and therein shall endeavour to humour the several great Claimers of Government in the Church of Christ.

1. I shall begin with a Monarchy. It's certain, his Holiness, either by reasonable Pleas, or powerful Cheats, has assumed an absolute and universal Sovereignty; this fills his Cathedral Chair, and is adorned with a Triple Crown, and in Defence thereof does protest. *The Almighty has made him both Key-keeper of Heaven and Hell, with the adjacent Territories of Purgatory, and vested in him an absolute Sovereignty over the Christian World.* And his Right has so far prevailed, that Princes and Civil Monarchs hold their Crowns and Donations as his Dutiful Sons, and Loyal Subjects; he therefore decks himself with the Spoils of the Divine Attributes, styling himself *Our Lord God, Optimum Maximum et supremum numen in Terris;* a God on Earth, a visible Deity, and that his Power is absolute, & his Wisdom infallible. And many of the great Potentates of the Earth have paid their Fealty, as tho' it was really so. One of them Clad in Canvas, going Bare-foot in the depth of Winter, [in Obedience to the Decree, stinting the Penance in proportion to the Wickedness of Princes] has waited many days for absolution at pious Gates. Another his thrown himself down prostrate a humble Penitent before him: He has placed his Holy Foot on the Monarch's profane Neck as

45

crushing a Vermine, crawling out of the Stable of his Sovereignty; and others frequently kiss his Toes with very profound Devotion. These and such like Triumphant Signals of his Sovereign Power does he wear. And indeed if he is the Universal Monarch of the Catholick Church, Princes that are Members of it must needs knock under; for that in one World there can not possibly be two *Most High's,* anymore than two *Infinites.* Thus, you see the Clergy, or Gospel Ministry of the Christian World have so wisely handled business, and managed the Gospel, that they have fairly [as they avouch] found a Sovereign Power bequeathed in it to the Ministry of Christ, and romaging more warily and nicely, at last, found a Spiritual Monarch, very compleatly furnished with the Keys of all sorts of Power hanging at his Girdle; and may we not pronounce the wiser they! seeing the World growing weary of Religion, was willing to loll it self down to Sleep, and leave them in sole Trust with the whole Interest of God's Kingdom. But the sad Enquiry is, Whether this sort of Government has not plainly subverted the Design of the Gospel, and the end for which Christ's Government was Ordained, *viz.* the Moral, Spiritual, and Eternal Happiness of Men?

But I have no occasion to pursue this Remark with tedious Demonstrations: It's very plain, it is written with Blood in Capital Letters, to be Read at Midnight by the Flames of *Smithfield,* and other such like consecrated Fires. That the Government of this Ecclesiastical Monarch has instead of Sanctifying, absolutely Debaucht the World, and subverted all good Christianity in it. So that without the least shew of any vain presumption we may Infer, That God and wise Nature were never Propitious to the Birth of this Monster.

An Aristocracy which places the Supream Power in a Select Company of choice Persons. Here I freely acknowledge were the Gospel Ministry Established the Subject of this Power, *viz.* To Will and Do, in all Church Affairs without controul, &c. This Government might do to support the Church in its most valuable Rights, &c. If we could be assured they would make the Scripture, and not their private Will, the Rule of their Personal and Ministerial Anions: And indeed upon these terms any Species of Government, might serve the great design of Redemption; but considering how great an Interest is imbarkt, and how frail a bottom we trust, though we should rely upon the best of Men, especially if we remember what is in the hearts of

46

Good Men, [*viz.* Much ignorance, abundance of small ends, many times cloked with a high Pretence in Religion; Pride Skulking and often breeding revenge upon a small affront; and blown up by a pretended Zeal; Yet really and truly by nothing more Divine then Interest, or ill Nature] and also considering how very uncertain we are of the real goodness of those we esteem good Men; and also how impossible it is to secure the Intail of it to Successors: And also it we remind how Christianity by the foresaid Principle has been peel'd, rob'd and spoiled already, it cannot consist with the Light of Nature to venture attain upon such Perils, especially if we can find a later way home. More Distinctly.

It is very plain [allowing me to speak Emblematically] the Primitive Constitution of the Churches was a Democracy, as appears by the foregoing Parallel. But after the Christian Churches were received into the favour of the Imperial Court, under the Dominion of Constantine the Great, there being many Preliminaries which had furnished the Ministers with a disposition thereunto, they quickly deprived the Fraternities of their Rights in the Government of the Churches, when they were once provided of a plentiful maintenance through the Liberality of *Constantine,* that when Christianity was so Luxuriantly treated, as by his great Bounty, and Noble settlement, it is said there was a Voice heard from Heaven, saying. *Now is Poyson poured into the Church*. But the subversion of the Constitution, is a story too long now to tell. Take therefore part of it, out of a late Author well versed in Antiquity, which may give some brief Image of the whole.

Non Multa secula jus Plebis Illasum Mansit, neque Aliter Evenire Potuit, Quin Illud, vel amitatur, vel saltem diminuatur, &c. De Ordina; Diff. Hystorica. P. 36. 40. 41.

The Right of the People did not remain unhurt through many Ages; neither could it well be other ways, but that it must be lost, or much diminished. *Zonaras* does confess that heretofore Bishops were chosen by the Suffrage of the People. But many Seditions happening among them; it was Decreed that every Bishop should hereafter be chosen by the Authority of the Bishops of every Province. The cause seemed to be so very specious, that nothing could be more Decent, or more Conducive to the safety of the Common-Wealth.

Yet, says my Author, if you do well weigh the business, you must needs acknowledge nothing could have happened more Pernicious or Destructive to the Church of God. For soon after these things came to pass, it is very obvious, that Tyranny over the Consciences of the faithful; and an Intolerable Pride every where grew Rampant among the guides of the Church. Yet there was one thing still very needful to be done; and that was to Establish or Confirm the Power which the Metropolitans and Bishops had acquired to themselves. Therefore they fell to it Tooth and Nail to drive away the Fraternity from all Interest in Elections: And alas Poor hearts! They began to sleep with both Ears; that then was scarce any enemy left to Interrupt, or Controul the Conquerors. This was the manner of the Clergy till they had made themselves the Subjects of all Power and then aded Arbitrarily, and did what they pleased in the Church of God.

But let the learned, knowing World, consider, what the issue of all this was, *foil.* what a wretched capacity the drowsiness & cowardice of the People; and the Usurpation and Ambition of the Ministry brought the Professing World into. If those who were truely Godly on both sides had in a few Ages lookt down from Heaven, and had Eyed the following Centurys, they might have beheld a world of matter for sorrowful Impressions; to think that they themselves had Occasioned the Ruin of Millions, by their remits and passive temper in one fort; and too much humouring, and nourishing Pride, and high conceits of themselves and others, in the other; when as if they had stood firm to the Government as left settled by the Apostles; they had certainly prevented an Apostasy that has damned, and confounded a great part of about Thirty Generations of Men, Women, and Children. That for my own part I can upon Experience, in some measure truly lay [to the History of the Primitive Churches in the loss of their Government; and the Consequents which followed, when I am Impelled to repeat it to my self] as one *Eneas* said to Queen *Dido*.

Infandum Regina Jubes Renovare Dolorem
—— Quis talia fando
Temperet e Lacrimis! ——

So doleful a Contemplation is it to think the World should be destroyed by those Men, who by God were Ordained to save it!

In a Word, an Aristocracy is a dangerous Constitution in the Church of Christ, as it possesses the Presbytery of all Church Power: What has been observed sufficiently Evinces it. And not only so but from the Nature of the Constitution, for it has no more Barrier to it, against the Ambition, Insults, and Arbitrary measures of Men, then an absolute Monarchy. But to abbreviate; it seems most agreeable with the Light of Nature, that if there be any of the Regular Government settled in the Church of God it must needs be.

3. A Democracy. This is a form of Government, which the Light of Nature does highly value, & often directs to as most agreeable to the just and Natural Prerogatives of Humane Beings. This was of great account, in the early times of the World. And not only so, but upon the Experience of several Thousand years, after the World had been tumbled, and tost from one Species of Government to another, at a great Expense of Blood and Treasure, many of the wise Nations of the World have sheltered themselves under it again; or at least have blendished, and balanced their Governments with it.

It is certainly a great Truth, *foil*. That Man's Original Liberty after it is Resigned, [yet under due Restrictions] ought to be Cherished in all wise Governments; or otherwise a man in making himself a Subject, he alters himself from a Freeman, into a Slave, which to do is Repugnant to the Law of Nature. Also the Natural Equality of Men amongst Men must be duly favoured; in that Government was never Established by God or Nature, to give one Man a Prerogative to insult over another; therefore in a Civil, as well as in a Natural State of Being, a just Equality is to be indulged so far as that every Man is bound to Honour every Man, which is agreeable both with Nature and Religion, 1 Pet. 2. 17. *Honour all Men*. —— The End of all good Government is to Cultivate Humanity, and Promote the happiness of all, and the good of every Man in all his Rights, his Life, Liberty, Estate, Honour, &c. without injury or abuse done to any. Then certainly it cannot easily be thought, that a company of Men, that shall enter into a voluntary Compact, to hold all Power in their own hands, thereby to use and improve their united force, wisdom, riches and strength for the Common and Particular good of every Member, as is the Nature of a Democracy; I say it cannot be that this sort of Constitution, will so readily furnish those in Government with an appetite, or disposition to prey upon each other, or imbezle the common Stock; as some Particular Persons may be apt to do when set off, and Intruded with the same Power. And moreover this appears very Natural, that when the aforesaid Government or Power, settled in all, when they have Elected certain capable Persons to Minister in their affairs, and the said Ministers remain accountable to the Assembly; these Officers must needs be under the influence of many wise cautions from their own thoughts [as well as under confinement by their Commission] in their whole Administration: And from thence it must needs follow chat they will be more apt, and inclined to steer Right for the main Point, *viz.* The peculiar good, and benefit of the whole, and every particular Member fairly and sincerely. And why may not these stand for very Rational Pleas in Church Order?

For certainly it Christ has settled any form of Power in his Church he has done it for his Churches safety, and for the Benefit of every Member: Then he must needs be presumed to have made choice of that Government as should least Expose his People to Hazard, either from the fraud, or Arbitrary measures of particular Men. And it is as plain as day light, there is no Species of Government like a Democracy to attain this End. There is but about two steps from an Aristocracy, to a Monarchy, and from thence but one to a Tyranny; an able standing force, and an Ill-Nature, *Ipso facto,* turns an abfolute Monarch into a Tyrant; this is obvious among the Roman *Caesars,* and through the World. And all these direful transmutations are easier in Church affairs [from the different Qualities of things] then in Civil States. For what is it that cunning and learned Men can't make the World swallow as an Article of their Creed, it they are once invested with an Uncontroulable Power, and are to be the standing Oratours to Mankind in matters of Faith and Obedience? Indeed some very wise and learned Men are pleased to Inveigh, and Reproach the Notion of Democracy in the Church, which makes the *Cotu fidelium* or Community of the Faithful the first Subject of the Power of Government. This they say tends to *Brownism,* and abhorred Anarchy; and then say they upon such premises, it must needs follow that very Member of the Body must be an Officer; and then every one must Preach and Dispense the Sacraments, *&c.*

Reply. Certainly such Gentlemen, either designs to pose and baffle their Reader with fallacy; or they themselves never took up, or understood the true Ideas of the several species of Government; in that a Democracy is as Regular a form, and as particular as any other. For,

1. An absolute or limited Monarch can't manage the Power or Government Devolved upon him, without the great Officers of the Crown or a large Sett of Ministers; tho' possibly he may with quicker dispatch issue out his Decrees, yet he must Execute all by his Ministry. And why may not a Democracy be indulged the same Liberty? and this will prevent all Anarchy or Confusion most apparently. But,

2. The bitter Pill to swallow in this Doctrine of a Democracy in the Church, is the terrible power of Life and Death, or the accountableness of particular Members to the Assembly, and especially those in the Ministry; but yet this is agreeable with the Nature of the Constitution, and easily managed without Anarchy, or popular Confusion also, which would be made very Evident, if we should but run the parallel in all points between the Democracy of the State and Church. But nextly from the Premises, I shall

3. Infer, That if these Churches are not properly formed, yet are fairly Established in their present Order by the Law of Nature. And will they be advised, I would Exhort them to try who will be so bold as to dare to disseize them. A Monarchy has been tryed in the Church with a witness, but it has absolutely failed us. An Aristocracy in a deep Calm threw the Democracy Overboard, and took not only the Helm in hand, but seized Ship and Cargo as their Right and Title, but after some time brought all to Ship-wreck, and that in a good Harbour too.

A Democracy was the noble Government which beat out in all the bad Weather of Ten Moody Persecutions under the management of Antiquity. And this is our Constitution, and what can't we be pleased? This Constitution is as agreeable With the Light and Laws of Nature as any other whatsoever, as has been fairly laid down, and fully Evinced, and more accommodated to the Concerns of Religion, than any other. Therefore I shall now conclude my Demonstration with this brief Appeal to the common Reason of Mankind, viz.

How can it consist with the Honourable Terms man holds upon here on Earth; that the best sort of Men that we can find in the World; such men as are adorned with a double sett of Enobling Immunities, the first from Nature, the other from Grace, that these men when they enter into Charter-party to manage a Trade for Heaven, must *ipso facto* be clapt under a Government, that is Arbitrary and Dispotick; yea that carries the plain symptoms of a Tyranny in it, when the Light of Nature knows of a better Species, and frequently has made use of it? It wants no farther Demonstration, for it's most apparent, that Nature is so much Mistress of her self, that man in a Natural State of Being, is under God the first Subject of all Power, and therefore can make his own Choice, and by deliberate Compacts settles his own Conditions for the Government of himself in a Civil State of Being: And when a Government so Settled shall throw its self from its Foundations, or the Subjects of Sovereign Power shall subvert or confound the Constitution, they then degrade themselves, and so all Power returns again to the People, who are the first Owners, And what! Is Man become so unfortunate, degraded and debased, as to be without all Power in settling a Government over himself relating to the Matters of his Eternal Well-Being? Or when he comes back to a Father's House, must he fall into the Capacity of a meer passive Being, and be put under such Tutors, as can easily turn Tyrants over him, and no relief left for him in his own hands; this is certainly most repugnant to the Light of Nature, and very disagreeable with the liberty and free Genius of a Gospel State. Nay, In a word. If the Government of the Churches be settled by God, either in the hands of a Church Monarch, or Aristocracy, and the People are no ways the Subject of Church-Power. Nay, if they are not under Christ, the fountain of Power; then the Reformation so called, is but a meer Cheat, a Schism, and notorious Rebellion; neither is there room left for the least palliation, or shadow of Excuse, for the Reformers in renouncing their Obedience to their Publick Governours. And the Martyrologies which pretend to immortalize the same of eminent Heroes, must be changed into Chronicles, handing along an account of the just and deserved fate of a crew of Rebels against God and Government; for what business had such a Company of illiterate and crack brain'd fellows to meddle with their Rulers, or Examine into their Administrations? For if they have no right of Power in Government, they stand absolutely bound to yield a passive Obedience and Non Resistance, and if they are so hardy and daring as to oppose their lawful Rulers, the sharpest penalty in this World, is too easie for them; the Inquisition is but dallying and playing with them. Hell is their desert. But how it conies about that a state of Grace, when in want of a suitable Government, is become such a Vassal, and wise and cunning Nature is by her Creator intrusted, and adorned with more ennobling Prerogatives, I must leave; and resign unto those Learned Men to Solve, who plead for an Aristocracy in the Churches of Christ.

But to wind up the whole Discourse in a few words, I acknowledge many Objections may be here made, and several Questions of Moment might here fall under Debate, but having obtained what I have principally fought for, in traversing the paths of Nature, in the three following Particulars; therefore with them, and with one Objection answered; and also with some brief Improvement of the Grand Hypothesis in this Demonstration, I shall finish the Argument.

1. Three Particulars, or so many golden Maxims, securing the Honour of Congregational Churches.

Particular 1. *That the People or Fraternity under the Gospel are the first Subject of Power; or else Religion links the Dignity of Human Nature into a baser Capacity with relation to Ecclesiastical then it is in, in a Natural State of being with relation to Civil Government.*

Particular 2. *That a Democracy in Church or State, is a very honourable and regular Government according to the Dictates of Right Reason, And therefore,*

Particular 3. *That these Churches of* New-England, *in their ancient, Constitution of Church Order; it being a Democracy, are manifestly Justified and Defended by the Law & Light of Nature.*

2. The Objection. *The Plea from the Law of Nature for a Democracy in the Church is as forceable for any other Species of Government; because Nature is furnished with such a variety of Schemes as has been pleaded to: And why may not the wise Christian Nations take which likes them best?*

Anfw. We must distinguish between man left solely to the Direction of the law of Nature, and as the Subject of Revelation, wherein Divine Wisdom may interpose; and determine on some particular Species, without hurting or crossing the Law of Nature. Therefore,

1. I readily grant and acknowledge, a Christian People may settle What Species of Government they please, when they are solely left to determine by the Law of Nature, what Government m the Church they will have. But then we must remember, that by the Argument of Concession, the Power is originally in the People; and then our

own Case is secure and safe enough; both on the account of the Reversion of Power, and especially, for that the People the first Subjects of Power, have been pleased to settle a Democracy for their Government, in the Churches of this Country. And if after the peaceable Possession of about an hundred years, any persons can persuade them to alter their Government into any other Species, this wilt be less worthy of blame, then craftily, or unfairly to force it out of their hands.

2. It's granted, that according to the Light of Nature, there be various regular Models of Government; but if Divine Wisdom is pleased to interpose and over-rule Nature's agitations, and cast the Scales for this or that particular Form, Nature will be but fair mannered to submit to its Author and Rector. So that if we find that God has Disclosed his Mind by Revelation, that his Churches by the Subject of a Democracy, then all stand obliged to comply under a double Bond. And so we come under a proper Crisis to enquire in the next place for Scripture-evidence in the Justification of these Churches.

But before I proceed to it, I shall

3. Make some brief Improvement of the main *Hypothesis* in the Demonstration; that is to say, the Government of the Gospel Churches, but a Democracy, these Consequences must necessarily follow, *foil*.

1. *Conf.* That the Right of Convoking Councils Ecclesiastical, is in the Churches.

2. *Conf.* That such a Council has only Consultative, not a Juridical Power in it. A Juridical Power committed to such a Representative Body is both needless, and also dangerous to the distinct and perfect States they derive from. Conrpleat States settled upon a Body of immutable and imperial Laws as its Basis, may want Council; but to Create a new Subject of Juridical Power, is some way to indanger the Being of the Creators.

3. *Conf.* That all the Members of an Ecclesiastical Council, deriving from a Democracy are Subjects of equal Power. Whatever the Power is, the several Delegates must from the nature of the Government they derive from, be equal sharers in it. Democratical States, in their Representative Body can make but one House, because they have but one Subject of Supream Power in their Nature, and therefore their Delegates, let them be who or what they may

be, are under equal Trust; so that none can justly claim Superiority over their Fellows, or pretend to a higher power in their Suffrage Indeed, in such Kingdoms, where the Sovereign Power is distributed and settled in divers Subjects, that the ballance of Power may be more Even, for the safety of the whole, and of all parts under all Acts of Sovereign Power: From such a Settlement of Power, there arises several distinct States in the same Government, which when Convened as one Subject of Sovereign Power, they make different Houses in their Grand Sessions; and so one House or State can Negative another. But in every distinct House of these States, the Members are equal in their Vote; the most Ayes makes the Affirmative Vote, and most No's the Negative: They don't weigh the intellectual furniture, or other distinguishing Qualifications of the several Voters in the Scales of the Golden Rule of Fellowship; they only add up the Ayes, and the No's, and so determine the Suffrage of the House.

Demonstration III - *From Holy Scripture*

This Plea has with such variety of Argument, and Illustration, and by many Repetitions, been pursued, by a great Number of Persons eminent for Learning and Piety, that I might here very fairly release myself from chis task. But yet to compleat the Number of my Arguments, I will briefly sum up the Demonstration for the Readers' use under a few heads.

1. Head. It must needs be allowed, as a fundamental Principle relating to Government, that [under God] all Power is Originally in the People. No Man I think will deny it to be a very sound Principle in Civil Knowledge. But if any Man will, I imagine it is sufficiently set forth in the former Demonstration. And it is very plain that Religion does always Cultivate, and Increase rather than Diminish any of Natures just Prerogatives. That it must needs stand for a Paradox, or a Riddle not to be Expounded; if Man is more of a Slave by his Religion than by his Nature. But let us take a brief view of Man by Scripture Account under a Religious Notion, as the Subject of Grace, and he seems then not to have the least speck of Vassalage in him; but is represented as though Lord of himself and owner of Heaven and Earth both, 1 Cor. 3. 22. — *all are yours.*

And though its very certain that Man has greatly debased himself by his Apostasy yet shall God puts abundance of Honour upon him in his Reduction. As we may consider Man in a remark or two, under the measures of Divine Grace in restoring him to favour. First, God treats him as a Creature of a very Honourable Character, as free and at his own dispose. Or as though he were some high and mighty State placed at the Top of this Glob: Therefore he Courts him into an Alliance as though he were likely to yield great Honour to the Crown. *We are Ambassadors —— as though God did beseech you by us; we pray you in Christ's stead —— be reconciled to God,* 2 Cor. 5. 20. This is much the Tenour of God's Heralds in their Addresses of Capitulation. That certainly if God did not highly estimate Man, as a Creature Exalted, by his Reason, Liberty and Nobleness of Nature, he would not caress him as he does in order to his Submission; but rather with some peevish and haughty Monarch, or the Bloody *Mahomet,* send his demands at the Mouth of his Cannon. But instead of such harsh measures, they are treated with the highest Reason, attended with Lenity and great Acts of Condescension. Nay, Divine Menaces are frequently cloathed with such soft Language as this; *Turn ye! Turn ye! Why will ye 'Dy?* Yea under all impulsive means, which God Wisely and Graciously makes use of to gain Man's consent, he sets the Will to turn about it self without forcing it, that so man's Religion may be the free and candid Emanations of his Noble and Exalted Nature. But when God thus gained Man; may we rationally imagine that in Erecting his Trophies he will assign and make him over to some Petty and Arbitrary Potentates in matters of Religion? or settle him under a Dispotick Government as tho' he was the spoils of a spiteful War? No certainly, but Man must now be considered as some high Allie invested with more Power then ever. This would still be more evident if we should consider what Christ has done and how they stand Joynt Heirs with him in his Purchase and Kingdom, *Rom.* 8. 1, 16, 17.

2. Head. The Power placed in Man that enables him to manage Religious affairs, is not Sovereign, but limited and confined Power. (1.) All Laws are Enacted already, and, (2.) There is no Coercive Power needful in the Church. The highest Act in Administring Judicature, is Excluding a Person out of the Society. In the Church there is no fees or fines, *&c.* In Civil Empire to keep Mankind in any good *Daecorum,* there's much hard work to be done, in Peace and War;

under mein Process, and in Criminal Causes. There's forming of Armies, raising the *posse Comitatus,* building of Castles &c. Cropping of Ears, Chopping off of heads and what not! So that Civil Government has need of an Immense Power as well as Treasure, and to be cloathed with Brass, and Iron. But as for the Church of God, Faith, Prayers & Tears, are generally their best Weapons against the Hostility of Foreigners; & in the Government of their homeborn, it may be done by soft words, or hard words, 1 *Thes.* 5. 12. *Heb.* 3. 13.—10. 24. 25. So that the business does not require abundance of External force, or form of Government. That it's a Thousand pieties to make such a great noise and bustle in the World about Church-Power, as tho' the Subjects of it were to furnish Armies and Knives to encounter half the Potentates on Earth in defence of the Church. When alas good men! As to all Occasion for Power its quite another thing; and the Exercise of it generally fails within reach of an ordinary Reason. That certainly whatever the Right of the Brotherhood is as to the Original of Power; there cannot he abundance of bad Omens in allowing them some share in Church Judicatory.

3. Head. Power — this Word seems to be all thunder. But however; it is very Copious and may be applyed to God and his Creatures. It is predicable of the latter, in their differing Classes and Orders of Being, and none so weak but have some share of it. But to confine the Word to Polity, *&c.* It is by some thus defined. *viz.*

Power or Authority — Is that whereby a Man may claim, or challenge any thing to ones felt, without the Injury of another, upon a supposition: This is a true definition.

Query. *Whether Christian People may not claim or challenge the following Rights or Prerogatives without doing injury to any. viz.*

1. Whether if they are pleased [a suitable number of them] to enter into a Religious Society, by punctual and voluntary Compacts to support the Worship of God in the Worlds whether this may not be done without injuring any? and then

2. When so united, whether they may not chuse their own Officers. (3.) Discipline their own Members (4.) Represent themselves upon Proper Emergencies, by their Delegates; [all which are the Principle Pillars of a Democracy,] whether I say, they can't do all these, without injury done to any others? But to proceed a little farther in opening the Nature of Power. If we unite '*Dunamis* and

Exousia, viz. Strength of Nature, and Authority of Institution into one Proposition. Then Political Power may be thus defined, *foil.*

Power is an Ability, furnished with a Lawful Right to Act. Now upon a presumption of the validity of this Proposition; Power may be easily apprehended as vested in every Church, and in every Member and Officer of a Church, according to the Nature, Degree and Duty of each Subject of Power; and may act and exert their several Powers and Authorities without any Incongruity, or Interfering one with another.

4. Head. That a Gospel Church Essentially considered as a Body Incorporated, is the Subject of all Church Power. Though a Church thus considered cannot formally Exercise all Branches of Power belonging to it: Neither can the Subject of Sovereign Power itself exert all Acts of Power till fitted with proper Organs or a suitable Ministry, and yet it can't be denied but that all Power really, and all Acts of Power Virtually must needs be in it. And so in a Church.

Therefore as to Church Power in the Exercise of it, it may be distributed into what belongs (1.) To the Combination of many, *viz.* The Power of Judgment and Donation. Or, (2.) To what belongs to one or more let off for that end, *viz.* The Power of Office. This Distribution Mr. Hooker pursues with great Illustration. *Surv. P. 1. p.* Here I shall confine my self to the consideration of the Exercise of that Power which belongs to the Brotherhood in distinction to Office Power. Which Principle I shall pursue by evincing the Truths of the following Proposicion. *foil.*

That the Scripture does Warrant a Government in Gospel Churches, consisting of the Exercise of several distinct Powers Inherent in the Fraternity, in distinction to Office Trust. This may be Evinced,

1. By the Recitation of the several distinct Powers themselves.

2, By the Dignity which the Scriptures puts upon the Churches as free States, and Subjects of Power in distinction from their Officers.

1. By the Recitation of the several distinct Powers; both Preparatory to, and Resulting from, their Combination.

1. There is a Preparatory Power is them both as Rational and Sanctified Beings of forming themselves into Churches. This Affirmation seems to me as fully contained in the genuine sense of Scripture, as though written in some Divine *Manifesto,* in such terms as these, *viz.* Let this be proclaimed through all the Earth,

that I the Lord Jesus Christ, have invested all Holy and good Christian People, both by Nature and Grace with Power, to enter into Church Order, for the advance of my Name, and their own Edification. If we had such an Article in Scripture written in terms, we should have made great use of it in justifying our Constitution; for it plainly settles all Power Originally [under Christ] in the People. And then if such a Power or Faculty be in them when in separate parts, as to Assemble, and enter into solemn Engagements, and thereby to enter into a Church State; it necessarily follows that having imbodied they may easily go forward and provide for their own well-being. He that hath read the Gospel, and observed how many Churches are mentioned, without Notice taken, of the manner of their Origination, must needs allow the observation to be a fair Consequence from it. It being so agreeable with the Light of Nature.

2. The Powers Resulting from their Combination may be more distinctly Recited.

1. Power. The Election of Officers. Officers are for the well-being, and compleating of any State. There is no Regular Government can well subsist without them; theft are the Hands, the Eyes, the Ears and Feet of Government in Administration. To separate Qualifyed Persons to the highest Office Trust in a State, is by Civilians attributed to the Creating Power of Sovereignty. So that it must needs be a great Power belonging to the Church under this head, and that it is the Churches Prerogative I might Reason; *Ex Jure Superioritatis.* For that the Church is Superiour to its Officers; and not the Officers to the Church. For that Churches are not made for Officers, but Officers for Churches; therefore says the Apostle, 1 Cor. 3. 22. *All things are yours — whether Paul, or Apollos or Cephas,* But I shall principally depend upon the Example and Practice of the Apostolical Church under this head. It is a Celebrated saying of Cyprian in pressing *Acts* 1. 26 To confirm the Power of the People in chusing and refusing their Officers. *Plebs Christiana maxime potestatem habet, vel Dignos Sacerdotes Eligendi, vel indignos Recufandi.* The highest Power of Electing worthy Officers and Rejecting unworthy is in the People. For the whole Church, says Turrettinus ['*de Jure Vo.*] *Duos Eligit,* chuses two to undergo the Lot for the Apostleship, that they might supply the vacancy by the Death of *Judas, Act.* 1. 23, 26. And indeed it is contrary to all Civility and Reason to imagine the Apostles would be so trivial in their Ministry, or prodigal of

their own Authority, as to indulge the Fraternity in such actions, *viz.* such as Electing an Extraordinary Officer, if the Election of Officers did not belong to them. So in the choice of the Deacons mentioned, *Act.* 6: 2, 3, 5. *The twelve called the Multitude of the Disciples unto them, and said – 'Brethren look you out among Men, whom we may appoint over this Business. The saying pleased the whole Multitude and they chose Stephen &c.* It must needs be very surprizing, if the Apostles should thus signify, and Intrust the Brethren with a Prerogative of Electing these Officers, if the Power of Election was not Inherent in them. That unless any one can fairly make it out that the Apostles were either in Jest, or did they know not what, in directing the Brethren, to do as they did in the Recited examples; it must needs stand for a Truth, that the Power of Electing Officers is in the Fraternity of the Church, by the Judgment of Christ's Apostles.

2. Power Judicatory, *Mat.* 18. 15, 20. This Paragraph of Holy Writ, lays open a Scheme of Juridical Power in the Subject of it; that is the Church: And this is to be observed. That from the first Commencement of the Process to the final issue in the Execution of the obstinate Judgemental Member, all is to be ascribed to the Authority of the Church; for what business has one man to interrupt another in his Crimes and unlawful Pleasures, unless he has power so to do? And how comes one man to have power over another, unless Conquest, Hostility, or Compact, have made them liable, as Members of the same Community, or Subjects of the same Government? Therefore the offended Person, proceeding regularly for detecting a Delinquent, must needs be supposed to derive his power from the same fountain, *viz.* the Sessions where the Case is finally to issue by Execution. And the Subject of this Power is the Church. *Tell the Church.*

And moreover, let it be considered, That to speak by way of allusion, there be several Removes of the Action of Trespass, from one hearing to another; as tho' it go from an Inferiour to a Superiour Sessions, and that Christ was here in this Precept, settling Inferiour and Superiour Assizes in his Kingdom; And indeed there cannot be a wiser Scheme drawn up, that shall carry the aspect of more Grace, Love, Humility, tender regard to Honour, and also Justice then this; both for the encouragement of Religion, the awing of Spectators, and keeping the Church pure. But to proceed,

1. In making; out Process, the first Tryal is to be had at the Assizes of a nun's own intellectual Powers, Reason, Conscience, &c. being Assembled, are to Sit in Judgment, hear the Pleas, .and the Indictment being read and justified, must pass Sentence; and at this Bar the Case may be fairly Issued. *If he shall hear thee, thou hast gained thy Brother.* So that most certainly the Plaintiff has a right to enter his Case at this Sessions, and here we see it may be issued; then certainly this is a Branch of the Power of Judicature; otherwise an aggrieved person might expect a very severe Repulse from a sturdier Offender, for interrupting a man's repose of mind in his own actions. What saucy Clown is that? who dare challenge my Conscience with the Cognizance of any Crime? Bold-face! where's your Commission; *Who made thee a Ruler, Acts* 7. 27. In Civil Affairs particular men when injured, must not make bold to correct an ordinary Trespass upon their Persons, or Interests, but by Forms of Law; if they do, especially if by measures which are grievous, they may be Indicted themselves for disturbers of the Peace: That certainly this branch of the Text refers to a legal Bar, and lawful Power. So that the complaining Party may Commence his Suit with boldness, produce his Pleas, and demand Justice. But the critical Question is, *Who is Judge of this Court?* Certainly it is some Layman's Powers, supposed to be very competent Judges, as sufficiently skilled in the Rules of Court, and how to apply them. And why may not all the Judges contained in the whole Series of Judicatory laid open in this Text, be of the same sort? for that the Case is not so deep, but that the first Judges & Sessions it comes before, are supposed by our wise Saviour & Law-giver, capable fully to understand and traverse it ', and do Judgment and Judice upon it ^ and bring it to a final issue. But,

2. Upon a Defeat the Process goes forward, by removing the Suit by an Appeal to a more impartial Hearing. The next Sessions therefore by Review, is to consist of one or two of the Brethren. [*Take one or two more*] But possibly some may be ready to say, Ah! *We are like to have very good Justice, before so wise a Sessions!* Well, it is what Christ has appointed, and let us keep his Path, and it will bring us safe home; for that these persons are Commissionated by Christ, as capable Judges, and therefore are to Exercise one branch of the Power fixed in the Church. But when the Case is gone thus far

thro' the Law, and the adverse Party will not submit to the last Verdict that is brought in, the Case must be Removed again. For that,

3. It is allowed to have one Tryal more, and no more; and that is to be before the Church. *For if he hear not the Church, he shall be as an Heathen man, &c.* that is to say, the Church shall then Issue out Execution, which is the End of the Law.

Object. *But the great and stupendous Objection, which crosses our way, is, That the Governing Church is here meant; that is to say, The Presbytery in their Classes, and several Sessions, till you, come to the last Appeal?*

Answ. 1. It is very Unscriptural to force such an Interpretation on the Text, for if we consider the Etimology, and universal Acceptation of the word Church, the Objection will be found very defective, both in its Rhetorick and Divinity. There being no harbour for it, within the sence of *Farniby's* Tropes or Figures.: And as for its Divinity, let the Objection but Cite one Text more, wherein Church is mentioned, and Officers are intended, and we will Resign. But without it to yield so great an Interest upon so slender a Claim is repugnant to Justice and Honour. But,

2. How can Wise Men manage their Souls, or bring them into such a figure as to think that Christ should have such a far reach in his thoughts in such easie Cases as are plainly contained in the Text? The Notions in the Objections are plainly ridiculous to the Light of Nature, in that Civil Measures adjust according to the Degree and Nature of Suits and Cases. A Cause of *Twelve-pence* is Tryable by a single Justice, and one Appeal brings the Suit to the end of the Law. Indeed Cases which are of greater weight and value have a larger scope in the Law allowed them, *&c.* And what! Is there the least shaddow for a pretence that such Cases as are within our Text, *viz.*, such as may be Issued by one single Brother making his Suit to his Brothers Reason and Conscience, *&c.* or by two at the most, and that at the sole Charge of a few honest Pleas from the heads of Charity or Piety? I say, Are these Cases so Grand as to be Transmitted from one Classis to another, till they arrive at the chief Seat where the definitive Sentence is to be given forth? There is apparently some great fallacy in the Objection, or certainly our Blessed Saviour did not state his Cases right; for let us again consider, who must sign the Bill of Cost at last? or who must bear all the Charges of Writings, Witnesses, Travels of Horses and Men; and for all Ex-

pense of Time and Money, from the Sessions first mentioned, and so from Sessions to Sessions, and from Classis to Classis, until evil is brought to a final Issue? When as possibly the Original Writ of Process, or first Action, might not contain it real Civil Damage, a *Farthing* more than about a *Groat* or *Six-pence*. And what can we think that our wise Saviour would adjust his Settlements at no better a rate than this comes to? vah! proh Dolor! Men have plainly made a Fool of Mankind by corrupting this Text whereby they have set the Discipline of the Church at such a Charge, that Millions of Millions have run out in waste, to humour their Ambition; when as the wise and innocent Churches of God in their single Capacities would have done better Justice, and have drained nothing more from you, than some Tears of Contrition. For,

3. What is more natural, than to imagine a Church of Believers, with their sett of Graces, and common Prudence, [especially when under the influence of a Regular Ministry] should be held capable to Execute this Rule, according to the full sence of it; yea, that they bring the Delinquent in the Traverse of the Case, to the highest Censure. Indeed it must be acknowledged, that Excommunication, major or minor, is an awful Result of Authority, yet not really in every respect, and in all degrees quite so bitter as Death it self: And yet Death is very frequently dispensed to Capital Sinners, and that solely by the Verdict of their Peers, *viz.* Twenty four good & lawful men of the Vicinage, are in forms of Laws sufficient Judicatory to take away a Man's life, and the Venerable Bench of Judges must not Over-rule, but stand and say, *Amen*, in that good Justice is done in the World by such a small Company of illiterate Men, the Law having assigned them to this Service. To the foregoing Precept, let us joyn *Col.* 4. 17. 1 *Cor.* 5. 12. *Rev.* 2. 20. 1 *Thes.* 5. 14. *Gal.* 6. 1.

Now to conclude, Let the Reader lay all these Scriptures together, which contain Rules of Judicatory for the Churches; and then let him answer me with good reason if he can, and tell me why these Scriptures may not be esteemed the Churches *Magna Charta,* in matters of Censure and Judicature; as well as that be held such a Golden Rule in the Judicial Proceedings of *English* Government, mentioned in the Great Charter of *English* Liberties Chap. 29. *No Freeman shall he Taken or Imprisoned or be Disseised of his Free-hold, Liberty or free Customs, or he Out'-Law'd or Exiled, or any other ways destroyed, nor will we press upon him, nor condemn him, but by lawful Judgment of his Peers.* Now Gentlemen! Don't you think that the Lord Jesus Christ, the King of Heaven, is as careful and tender of his Subjects, as the King of *England* is of his? And indeed, why should not each sett of Subjects be equally and alike guarded from the hazzard of Oppression, or the Arbitrary Measures of each Ministry? unless those that belong to the Gospel, are formed out of a Distinct Clay from each other?

3. Power. To represent themselves in Synodical Conventions, for the Establishment of this Power in the Churches. See *Acts* 15. 2. 22, 23. And for a more ample Display and Consummation of this Point, I Refer the Reader to the Excellent Treatise of Dr. *Increase Mather,* in His Disquisition concerning *Ecclesiastical Councils,*

2. The Dignity which the Scripture puts upon the Churches as Free States, and Subjects of Power in distinction from their Officers.

It is very plain that most of the Epistles of St. *Paul* which make up a great part of the Canon of Scripture, were directed to the Body of the Brotherhood, and peculiarly adapted for their use, with little or no Notice to all taken of the Ministry therein,

In sum, when he was just concluding his Letter and winding up his Discourse with his Grace and Respects to some choice Christian Friends, he puts the Officers in with them, and Orders the Brotherhood to give his Salutations to them as Persons unconcerned with the Contents of the Epistle, *Heb.* 13. 24. In the last Verse but one in the whole Epistle, says the Apostle, *Salute all them that have the Rule over.* That what ever other meanings may be in such Methods of Divine Writings, they must needs Respect some high Powers and Trust vested in the Churches. Those Epistles sent to the Angels of the Churches of *Asia;* the Principal share of those Letters, litterally taken, which belonged to the Officers, is but the Superscription; the Contents of the Letters are immediately directed to the Fraternity. Where there is any thing amiss the Fraternity is Reprehended: Where there is any thing worthy of Credit, they are Commended. Or if there is anything in point of Order or Discipline to be done they are directed and Commanded. All is to the Churches. Therefore it is said again and again, *He that hath an Ear to hear, let him hear what the Spirit saith unto the Churches,* Rev. i. 7. &c. Finally, Let any considerate Man but read and well ponder the Epistles to the *Corinthian, Ephesian,* &c. Churches, and observe the Characters of the Brotherhood; with the Precepts how they shall Act Personally and with Authority one towards another &c. he must then needs subject of his mind to the force of this Conclusion, *foil*. That Christ's Gospel Churches is their Fraternities, are not such Cyphers as they stand in some Men's accounts; but are really and truly proper Bodys full of Powers, and Authorities, for the Government of themselves and all their concerns, as all Democracys are.

Demonstration IV.

From the Excellent Nature of the Constitution, in that it exceeds all that have been yet Extant in the Christian World. This I shall endeavour to Illustrate by three Pleas.

Plea. I.

In that it best suits the Great and Noble Designs of the Gospel, and that in a peculiar manner as it tends to the promoting Holiness in the World; not only from the strict Nature of the Constitution in the Admission of Members, whence the Churches become a more exact Emblem of Heaven, both for the illuminating and dreading of others, that beholding their Goodness, may Glorify God in the day of Visitation. 1 *Pet*. 2. 12. But from the great advantage put into the hands of the best sort of men, [solid, pious, wise and unbyas'd men] of furnishing a Country with Persons eminently Qualified for the Ministry, and keeping them so. There is no lurking-place for *Symony* in the Constitution. There is no buying and selling of Offices, whereby the World has been miserably cheated, and debauched. Here is no back Stairs for Cousins and Favourites to Climb up to high Seats without Desert; it is merit and intrinsick Worth sets the value, and holds the strongest plea for Preferment here. Hence every Village, and corner of a Town, where Religious Congregations are Settled, are furnished with Persons for the Gospel Ministry of such Learning, and bright Saints, and of such real and distinguishing Vertue and Zeal, that they must needs be very prevalent in carrying on the main design, *&c*. But this Plea is fully pursued by Dr. *Owen,* in his Enquiry, *&c*. [p. 120 and so on] whither I refer the Reader that wants more satisfaction.

Plea II.

For that it has the best ballance belonging to it of any Church Government in the World. Other Governments have generally too high a Top, and are very lopsided too: Nay the best we can meet with without vanity or Envy it may be said, that not only seemingly like *Grantham* Steple, but really it stands awry, and being so over loaded on Natures corrupt side, with Learning, Power and high Trust it plainly hangs over several Degrees from a true perpendicular, towards *Babylon:* And if it falls it burys you; and then you must remember it has Monopolized all Power, so that you have none left to stir under your load, or creep out with. But here's a Government so exactly poyzed, that it keeps its Motions Regular like the stupendous Spheres, unless some *Phaeton* chance to mount the Chariot Box, and becomes the driver. I have sufficiently, I think, evinced the Power in the Brotherhood; and though every Church is a Body consisting of very numerous Parts and a noble Ministry, yet the ballance of Power is very exactly and with great advantage preserved; both between the Members of the Body in general, and between themselves, and their Publick Ministry in special.

1. Between the Members of the Body. For besides, the Wisdom, Love and other ennobling Principles, in some measure actuating every member. The Venerable Major Vote, which Guides and Governs the August States of Parliaments; my all Assembly's, Superiour and Inferiour, that have any Equality of Power dispersed amongst the Members, Ordinarily keeps the whole Body, in all points of Administration, in an exact Equipoize.

2. And as for the state of the Ministry there is no grain of allowance wanted on their side, to make their Office Power, if not an even ballance Arithmetically upon an accurate, and distressing Tryal: Yet in the series of a laudable Ministration, it is an Equivalent of Power; at least according to the terms of our Constitution, *Platf. C.* 10 *Sect.* 11. But let the case be stated as accurately as may be; and let every fair Principle which grants the Power to be Originally in the People, be yielded: and also Establish a proper Indicature in the Brotherhood, yet its apparent in all Examples, that the Ministry of this Constitution are held, if not in proper speaking; yet in Conscience, and Religious Courtesie, as though all Power were invested in them; or at least to such a Degree that there is no appearance of

what may render the Government grievous to them, it they are but contented, to be the Master of an Assembly of Free Men, and not of Slaves. Amongst abundance of Illustrations I will mention two.

1. The great Veneration in Man's mind towards those who are sensibly cloathed with Authority. *If I am a Father where's my Honour, if a Master where is my Fear, Mat.* 1. 6. The Prophet Reasons from the Law of Nature; there being such a property planted in the Soul by its Maker to revere superiours, and especially Men in publick trust. And also the Authority shining in them, being such bright Rays both of the Divine Majesty and Benignity, there being such a sensible Good and Benefit accruing thereby, to the rest of Mankind, hence springs a universal disposition to Obedience and Submission, this is obvious through the whole Civil Ministry of the World; there is no need to make every Judge in Commission, or chief Magistrate a Sovereign Prince to gain Homage to him. No! but as soon as a Man appears vested with Authority, there is that in the Soul of another which teaches Reverence and Obedience to him in his Trust, both from the Suggestions of fear and sence of Interest. So that a Learned, Painful and Pious Ministry Intrusted with the Souls & happiness of Men; and taking Indefatigable care to secure Eternal Life for them, has a most charming and endearing Aspect and Influence upon all the Rational Powers. In as much that Nature it felt has a high value for such Subjects of Trust. And as for Grace its ready to be lavish of its Victims. — ye — received me as an Angel of God even as Christ Jesus. — If it had been possible ye would have plucked out your own Eyes, and have given them to me, *Gal.* 4. 14, 15. If any Man doubts of the validity this Plea, let him but view what Conquests have been made by the abuse of these Principles, and you will find the Ministry of the Christian World have far exceeded *Caesar,* in subduing Mankind; for from an honest Obedience they have brought them to lie down, & be trampled on by their Spiritual owners. That there is no danger on the People's side when things are well stated, it there be but a wise and due management on the other. And still it is more evident.

2. From the Extent of Commission, with the many ennobling Prerogatives fixed in their Trust. Though they are the Ministry, and but the Ministry of a Democracy, their Commission is so Large, and High-Prerogatives so numerous, they Carry so great an appearance, as though in reality they were the Subject of all Power. And I think

it is so from the Nature and Modes of all Regular Government; for when a Government has Enacted their Laws and Precepts, and setled their Ministry, they leave the sway of things to them; that it is as though they had Resigned all the Power to their Ministry: So it is peculiarly in the affairs of Gospel Churches. That let men at their leisure view this Illustration by the scripture, our Platform, and by the Laws and Customs of Nations, and they will find it a Truth. That certainly a painful Ministry may easily be reconciled to our Constitution, unless they are raised to that Temper of mind as he was, who had this for his Motto, *Aut Caesar aut Nihil,* A *Caesar* or nothing.

Plea III.

From the near Affinity our Constitution holds with the Civil Governments of some of the most flourishing Common-wealths in the World. It's certain, every Species of Government simple and mixt, have their various Excellencies and Defects; much may be said in honour of each, and also every Constitution may have something wanting*, at least it may seem so, under a more critical survey of its Nature, Principles, Ill-conveniencies, corrupt Ministry, Misfortunes, &c. And many times a Government falls under Scandal from Distemper of Mind, from false Ends and corrupt Interests, which sway and overrule men's tho'ts relating to Government, more than from the Constitution it self. But however, to Evade all circular Discourses, we may very fairly Infer, where we find Nations flourishing, and their Liberty and Property, with the rest of the great Immunities of Man's Nature nourished, secured, and best guarded from Tyranny, we may venture to pronounce this People to be the Subjects of a noble Government, and there he many such on Earth, whole Constitution will serve to justifie ours. I shall instance in three, and no more.

1. The *Venetian* Commonwealth; tho' some are pleased to call the Government of this free State, an Aristocracy; but it seems more properly a limited Democracy; for that the Seat of Sovereign Power is their ancient Commons, called their Families, Enrolled in the Golden Book; these make up the grand Council of the Nation, settle the Publick Ministry. and Enact Laws, &c. This People have by this mode of Government railed themselves into so august and flourish-

ing a Capacity, that from a very obscure Original, they are grown to that degree, as to bridle and curb the pride and haughtiness of *Turk* and *Pope*. This Example must needs be no small Honour to our Constitution. But,

2. The *Belgick* Provinces are without Interruption allowed to be the Subjects of a formed Democracy, They in some Ages past being insulted, and unmercifully trampled upon by that august Tyrant, the *Spanish* Monarch; they being his Subjects broke loose from him, and set up for themselves. They assumed to themselves their Original Power, and when they had got it into their hands, had the wit, and kept it, and have improved it in the form of a Democracy to this day, and God has blest them: That from the poor States of *Holland*, they are now grown to wear the splendid Title of *Their High Mightinesses*, and are a Match for most Monarchs on Earth. Says *Gordon* of their Government: *The seven Province of* Holland *being under a Democratical Government, art as it were several Commonwealths; each Province being a distinct State; yea, and every City having an Independent Power within itself to Judge of all Causes, whether Civil or Criminal, and to inflict even Capital Punishments; but all joyning together, make our Republich, the most considerable in the World.*

Query. *Whether such Examples of Popular Government now Extant on Earth, and yielding such vast advantages to the Subjects, and being so regular and practicable; I say, whether they may not justly deter all men from reproaching our Constitution with the scandalous Title of Anarchy, unless they will allow us to prepare a Chronicle for them, and therein publish to the World their profound Ignorance of the several Species of Governments; and the distinct way of Placing and Exercising various Powers in them.*

3. The *English*. This Nation is reputed to be the Subject of the finest And most incompatible Government in the World. And this Original happy Form of Government, Is [says one] *Truly and properly called an* English *Man's Liberty: A priviledge to be freed in Person and Estate from Arbitrary Violence and Oppression; and a greater Inheritance than we derive from our Parents.* And this Birthright of *English* Men shines most conspicuously in two things.

1. In *Parliaments;* wherein the Subject has by his Representatives, a share in Legislative Power; And so makes his own Laws, and disposes of his own Money.

2. In *Jury's;* whereby he has a share in the Executive pare of Law, so that no Causes are Tried, nor any man Adjudged to lose his Life, Member or Estate, but upon the Verdict of his Peers; his Equal or Neighbours, and of his own Condition. These two grand Pillars of English Liberty, are the fundamental vital Priviledges whereby we have been, and are still preserved more free and happy, than any other People in the World; and we trust shall ever continue. For whosoever shall design to impair, pervert, or undermine either of theft, do strike at the very Constitution of our Government, and ought to be prosecuted and punished with the utmost zeal and vigour. For to poyson all the Springs and Rivers in the Kingdom, could not be a greater mischief; for this would only affect the present Age, but the other would Ruine and Inslave all our Posterity. I shall improve this Example by three Queries.

Query 1. Ah! What's the matter with *English* Men of such Courage to be surprized with such fear, as tho' they were like to be taken Captive, and turned into Slaves in their own Home? Why, in good truth, there may be a Reason for it; therefore it becomes them to be very careful under this head; for if they make themselves Slaves in their own Country, or let others do it for them, when they can prevent it, they both deny God who Made and Redeemed them, and plainly Violate the Law of Nature?

Query 2. Who is it *English* Men are thus afraid of? Who do they thus Reflect upon in their frights and fears? It is neither *France* not the *Great Turk* which dreads them! therefore it must needs be some body or another nearer home that threatens their Liberty. And may not *New-England's* Gospel Liberties deserve so much fear and caution, although it should so happen that some body should be Reflected up on by their Cautiousness.

Query 3. If the settling such Immunities, as the priviledge of Parliaments and Juries in the hands of the People be such effectual Barriers to preserve a Nation from Tyranny and Slavery; then whether when Gospel Churches have the Means in their own Power, it been't their wisdom to keep up the like Barrier, or something equivalent thereto; that they may preserved themselves safe from the Arbitrary Measures of their own Ministry? or thus, Whether for *English* Men, when their Liberties in Church or State are fast lockt up for them and their Posterity by Law and regular Settlements, It been't their best way to beware how they Repeal those Laws, or weaken those Settlements?

But at present I shall leave it to other men to fan the Parallel between our Constitution, and the several Governments I have mentioned, and infer what more they shall think proper, only leaving to myself the liberty to conclude, that the several Examples of Civil States, which I have named, do serve abundantly to justifie the noble Nature of our Constitution in Church Order; for that the several famous & august Nations which I have mentioned, in all their Glory at Home, & Success in Arms & Trade Abroad; their several Governments which have brought them to all this, are either a perfect Democracy, or very much mixed and blendished with it.

Then why should we in *New-England* be any more ashamed, or less careful of our Church-Government, which keeps us from Tyranny and Slavery in the concerns of our Consciences, then those Nations are of their Civil Government, whereby they are preserved from the like damnable Circumstances in the Concerns of their outward Life and Natural Rights and Fortunes?

Demonstration V.

From the Dignity which the Providence of God has put upon the Constitution, both in the first Ages of the Christian Churches, and in the last Century.

1. In the first Ages of the Christian Churches God has put many Marks of distinguishing Favour upon this Constitution, both in the smiles and frowns of his Providence.

1. In the smiles of Providence upon the Churches, whilst they continued compleat in their Constitution. I shall offer but three Particulars, to justifie this *Observation*.

1. In the great and admirable success of the Gospel, in the *Conversion* of so many Nations.

2. In their singular Purity, and *Vertuous Deportment* in the midst of a corrupt World. That [as *Mr. Cotton* observes] *was a general Eulogy belonging to their Members, and ascribed to them by the wiser sort of Heathen*, foil. *Bonus vir, tantum Christianus,* He is a Good Man only is a Christian.

3. They were eminently supported & carried On by the Grace & Providence of God thro' all their direful Sufferings; the more they were wasted and destroyed, the more they grew and increased, as *Israel* in *Egypt.* Indeed whilst they remained firm to their Constitution, they were not only like an Army in Banners, but in reality the greatest Conquerours that ever appeared on Earth. They meerly baffled the bravery of the old *Roman* Spirit, and were quite too hard for those who had vanquished the World. I have seen, saith *Eusebius,* the Executioner [tyred with tormenting them] *lie down panting and breathing,* &c. But I never saw the Martyrs weary of Sufferings, nor heard them desire Truce: Nay, were rather ambitious of the longest and most terrible Sufferings, that they might be Martyrs in every Member. Thus the Churches endured hardness as good Souldiers of Christ, thro' ten bloody Persecutions; and at last Retreated by Divine Providence, under the Umbrage of the Great *Constantine.* And there the Churches of God made the finest show that ever was seen on Earth, next to Christ in his Transfiguration. Till this time the Churches remained the Subjects of their Democratical Government in some good measure tho' there were some symptoms of an alteration in the last Century, but indeed after the Churches were freed from the rage of Heathen Persecutors, there quickly followed the perfect subversion et their Order. So we come,

2. To Consider the frowns of Providence hat pursued the Christian World after the Subversion of their Primitive Constitution. Sufficient observations have been made under foregoing Demonstrations, setting forth the Change of Government which was made in the Churches. And in short, it was really and properly the altering the Ministry of a Democracy into an Aristocracy; for to speak plainly, the Publick Officers to gratifie their ambition, took all the Power into their own hands, and settled all Affairs and Concerns according to their own minds without controul. But let us Eye the Providence of God, and we may observe that God did soon stain the pride and glory of these men; especially in two eminent instances of His Displeasure, which I shall only mention.

Instance 1. In the fatal *Arian* Heresy, that spread it self like some mortal Contagion, thro' the Christian World; that it was said the whole World was become an *Arian. Arius* was the Author of this Damnable Doctrine, *viz.* That our Saviour Christ was neither God, nor Eternal, but a *Creature;* and that he assumed only the Body, not the Soul of Man, &c. This Damnable Heresy soon spread it self far and wide; the Author was in the heighth of his wickedness, and fell a Victim to Divine Vengeance in the latter part of *Constantine's* Reign: But his Heresy continued and prevailed, and especially amongst the Clergy. But this is very awful to observe, That when these men by their wit and cunning had once coufened and cheated the Fraternity of their ancient Rights and Prerogatives, God left the Devil to cheat and deceive them, as Wise and Learned as they were, of their true Religion and Souls together. What good did all their Legerdemane do them now? had not they better have kept holy and humble Pastors, confined to their Parochial Dioceses, and known and Loved and Preach't Christ the Eternal Son of God, and him Crucified, rather then stretcht their Boundary like Sovereign Princes, and so left to perish under such a dreadful Dispensation, as the fruit of their Ambition and Infidelity?

To me, [considering the Commencement, the deadly Nature, the Rage, the universal Prevalence and Continuance of this damnable Heresy] it seems as though God had lookt down from Heaven, and viewed the Sacrilegious Robbery committed upon the Churches with Detestation. And therefore summoned a Congress of the several States of the other. World. [1 King. 22. 19. *I saw the Lord sitting on his Throne*] and issuing out Proclamation. — *Be it known! That never has a Nobler Cause been so baffled and Sacrilegiously betrayed by the Dignified Trustees of it as this. I have been down amongst my Golden Candlesticks, my famous Churches; I find the Fraternity drowsie and remiss, setting too low a value on their inestimable rights. And those who should rowse them from their Security and Incogitancy, rather steem it a Lucky Omen; and therefore to satiate their own Ambition [instead of advising, and directing the Churches in the study of their Constitution; and so plead their Cause for them] they consult how to defraud them, they wrest the Scripture, darken all places which settle their titles, and to end all disputes threaten them* Diotrephes *like* [3 Joh. 10.] *with the secular power that is now on their side. That they have at last absolutely supplanted them, stript and taken away the Rights belonging to the Churches, and purchased it so dear a Rate. That as though the Almighty should say, my Patience is out! And my Justice has prepared a Cup of Confusion for them; Who! if all this Convocation will go and hand it to them; And there came forth several Legions with an Arch-Devil at the head of them, And flood before the Lord, and said, we will go and persuade them; and God said, you shall persuade them, and prevail also;* therefore go forth and do so, 1 King. ii. 22. As though God should say, I have now in displeasure abandoned them to Ruin; they who should have had a zealous regard to my settlements; and as one Chief end of their Ministry, should have fought the happiness of the People, and not their own ease, vain Glory, Pride and Luxury: now leave them exposed to obliterate the Essentials of their Faith, and so fall a Sacrifice to Divine fury. Go you malignant Powers do your worst, the Hedges are now down.

Instance 2. The universal Apostasy that has followed the subversion of the Old Constitution. We may in some degree date God's departure from his Churches when they began to subvert the order of them, and so gradually withdrew, till he ---- at last left them to perish by whole Ages together. It must not, indeed, be thought, or said, but that God had a Remnant through many Ages, who continued Orthodox in Faith, both in the Ministry and Brotherhood. But yet it is very obvious that Christianity *Gradaim*, declined till all was swallowed up in a Universal and Direful Apostasy, never sufficiently to be deplored, neither fully Exprest, unless we Transcribe the Volumns that contain it. I do account indeed that the destruction of the Churches, in moral speaking, may be attributed immediately and nextly to other Causes, as Ignorance, Pride, Hypocrisy, &c. But remotely to the dissolution of the Order of them. For that the Constitution forenamed was adjusted by Divine Wisdom for preventing and remedying such Maladies as proved; the ruin of the Churches; that when the remedy was quite taken away, bad Humours Predominate, & Symptoms of a deadly Aspect appear, and so Death inevitably follows.

2. In the last Century God has been very Admirable in the works of Providence, and has therein highly Dignifyed our Constitution. And we want no other evidence under this head then the Recognition of what God has done for these famous *English* Colonys in North-America; who have all along distinguished themselves, from all the World, by their singular regard both to the Faith and Practice of the true Religion. Now let any other Constitution on Earth but Parallel ours; in the eminent shines of Providence and in Religious Effects, and we will resign the whole Cause. But whilst then, we will go on, and rejoyce in the Grace of God, that we in these

Countrys, are by his good Providence over us, the Subjects of the most Ancient, Rational and Noble Constitution in Church Order that ever was, will be, or can be; whilst the Laws of Nature and Grace remain unrepealled. For that it is a Constitution which Infinite Wisdom hath Authorized and founded in the Law of Nature; and his Omniscient Providence has eminently Honoured, and Dignifyed, both by the Smiles and Frowns of his Countenance, through all the Ages of the Christian World to this very Morning. And though some of the Reverend Churches within this and Consociation [who settled upon the same Platform with us] have with too great a Precipitation made a Defection from the Constitution: Yet this is our Comfort, that their alteration is not so firm, as the Laws of the *Medes* and *Persians;* for that those who turn'd them off, may by the same Power bring them on to their old Basis again. And let Christ pity, and help them, For certainly their present State is Portentous, from what may be observed from the Proceedings of Providence through the whole Christian Aera, unto this Day.

The Conclusion.

I shall now Conclude my whole Essay, by annexing the Joynt Testimony of those eminent Men, Fathers In these Churches, now in Glory. *viz.* The Reverend Mr. *John Higginson,* and the Reverend Mr. *William Hubbard.* And the rather because Mr. *Hubbard* did some time before his Death, desire to have their Testimony Reprinted, and Live with some other Book which it might properly accompany,; am well satisfyed the foregoing subject is the most proper Companion, their Testimony could have Light on, in its Travels through the World: I therefore make bold to invite the said Testimony, to set out again with fresh Courage, and improve its Excellent Language, together with former acceptance it found with the Churches, to ingratiate and bespeak favour for this small Treatise, its new Allie and Fellow-Traveller.

And let the Holy Churches [for whom these now appear in Joynt Testimony, to confirm their Divine Pedigree] flourish in their Strength, Beauty and Order, after this Triumvirate shall sink under the Tyranny of Moths, and Humane forgetfulness, and lye down in the House of oblivion; where I hope the Enemies of the Constitution will be gotten down before them, and there last Buried in their own Bones and Dust.

But least any should think it absurd, that I here produce such Venerable Authority in way of Epilogue, which should rather in Honour have been placed in the front of this attempt. To this I reply, that in Honour and Prudence I chuse here to place these Worthies. For you must note; I am now Retreating out of the field of Battle, and I hope upon Honourable terms too; and then the Reer is the highest place in dignity; so that though they are bringers-up, its no diminution to them. And not only so, but out of Prudent Conduct; for though I presume the Enemy is fairly Vanquished, yet some forlorn party may rally, and to gratify their desperate fortune may disturb us, but I hope these valiant and wise Commanders thus posted, will secure our Reer, beat back the Enemy, and bring all off with Triumph.

FINIS.

A Testimony

To the *Order of the Gospel,* in the Churches of New-England: Left in the Hands of the Churches, by the two most Aged Ministers of the Gospel, yet surviving in the Countrey.

I. Above *Seventy Years* have passed away, since one of us, and above *Sixty,* since the other of us came into *New-England,* and *having obtained Help from God, we continue to this Day.*

We are therefore capable to make some *Comparison,* between the Condition of the Churches, when they were first Erected in this Countrey, and the Condition into which they are now *Fallen,* and more *Falling* every day.

But we wish, that in making this *Comparison,* we had not cause to take the place, and the pare of those *Old Men,* that saw the *Young men shouting aloud for Joy, at the New Temple,* Ezra. 3. 12. *Ancient men that had seen the First House; when the Foundation of this House was Laid before their Eyes, Wept with a Loud voice.*

2. We are under a daily Expectation of our call to appear before our Lord Jesus Christ; and we have reason to be above all things concerned, that we may *give up our Account with Joy* unto Him That we may be the better able to do so, we judge it necessary for us, to leave in the Hands of the Churches, a brief Testimony, to *the Cause of God, and His People* in this Land. And this the rather, because we are sensible that there is Risen and Rising among us, a Number who not only forsake the *Right wayes of the* Lord, wherein these Holy Churches have walked, but also labour to carry away as many others with them as they can.

We are also informed, that many *Younger men* of great worth, and hearty Friends unto the *Church-State* of the Country, scarce know what Interpretation to put upon it; but find it a sensible Disadvantage unto them, that the *Elder Men* are so silent, and remiss upon the manifest occasions, that call aloud for us to open Our *Mouth* in the cause of Churches that we should be loth to *see Led unto Destruction.*

3. We that saw the Persons, who from Four Famous Colonies, Assembled in the *Synod,* that agreed on our *Platform of Church Discipline*, cannot forget their Excellent Character. They were Men of Great Renown in the Nation, from whence the *Laudian Persecution* Exiled them; their Learning, their Holiness, their Gravity, struck all men that knew them with Admiration. They were *Timothies* in their Houses, *Chrysostomes* in their Pulpits, *Augustines* in their Disputations. The *Prayers,* the *Studies,* the Humble *Enquiries,* with which they fought after the mind of God, were as likely to prosper as any mens upon Earth. And the *Sufferings* wherein they were *Confessors* for the Name and the Truth of the Lord Jesus Christ, add unto the Arguments which would persuade us, that our Gracious Lord would Reward and Honour them, with Communicating much of His Truth unto them. The Famous *Brightman* had foretold, *Clariorem lucem adhuc Solitudo dabit, &c.* God would yet Reveal more of the true Church-State unto some of His Faithful Servants, whom He would send into a *Wilderness,* that He might there have Communion with them. And it was eminently accomplished in what was done for and by the *Men of God,* that first Erected Churches for Him in this *American* Wilderness.

We do therefore in the first place, Earnestly *Testifie,* That if any who are given to Change, do Rise up to Unhinge the *well Established* Churches in this Land, it will be the Duty and Interest of the Churches, to examine, whether the men of this *Trespass,* are more *Prayerful,* more *Watchful,* more *Zealous,* more *Patient,* more *Heavenly,* more Universally *Conscientious,* and Harder *Students,* and better *Scholars,* and more willing to be *Informed* and *Advised,* than those Great and Good men, who left unto the Churches what they now enjoy: If they be *not so,* it will be *Wisdom* for the Children to forbear *pulling down with their* own *Hands,* the *House, of God,* which were Built by their *Wiser Fathers,* until they have better satisfaction.

It is not yet forgot by some surviving Esrwitnelles of it, that when the *Synod* had finished the *Platform of Church-Discipline* they did with an Extraordinary Elevation of Soul and Voice then Sing together, *The Song of Moses the Servant of God, and the Song of the Lamb,* in the fifteenth Chapter of the *Revelation:* God forbid, that in the loss of that Holy *Discipline* there should be hereafter occasion to Sing about *breaking down the Carved work of the Houses of God,* with *Axes and Hammers;* or take up the *Eightieth Psalm* for our Lamentations.

4. It was a Joy unto us, to See and Read, a Book which the Reverend Praesident of our Colledge lately Published, under the Title of *The Order of the Gospel, Professed and Practised by the Churches of Christ in New England:* A Book most highly needful, and Useful, and Seasonable; a most Elaborate and well-composed work, and well suited unto those two worthy designs; 1st, the maintaining the *Congregational Church Discipline;* and 2dly, the maintaining the sweet Spirit of *Charity* and *Communion* towards *Reforming Presbyterians,* who are our *United Brethren.* But we must herewithal *Testify,* that in that worthy Book, *there is nothing obtruded upon the Churches,* but what they who were here, capable of observing what was done Sixty Years ago, do know to have been *Professed and Practised in the Churches of New England;* (except in one or two) Then and ever since, until of late, some who were not then Born, have suggested otherwise. Yea, 'tis well known, that the Churches then Publickly maintained those Principles, in several judicious Discourses, which were never confuted by any men whatever, unto this present time. And we do therefore most Heartily commend that Book, of the *Order of the Gospel,* unto the perusal and acceptance of the Churches of the Lord.

5. It was one of the *Songs* (as the Jewish Masters tell us) in the Feast of Tabernacles, *Blessed be our Youth, which have not made our Old Men ashamed.* But alas, we that are *Old men* must confess ourselves *Ashamed,* when we see after what manner some of our *Youth,* have expressed and behaved themselves, and with what Scoffs they have assaulted the *Order of the Gospel,* in some things lately Published, and Scattered about the Country: Which have been so far from Answering the *Arguments* brought for our *Church Order.* That they have been by the wonderful Providence of Christ, made useful to Establish the minds of Serious Christians, in those very points, which they see so weakly and so rudely opposed. We have taught our Children in the *Catechism,* called *Milk for Babes,* that there is to be a *Covenant of God* in the Churches, wherein *they give up themselves, for unto the Lord to be his People, and then to the Elders and Brethren of the Churches to set forward the Worship of God, and mutual Edification,* And it cannot but be grievous unto us, as well as unto all serious Christians, for my *Children* of *New-*

England, Scornfully to vomit up their *Milk* with *Scoffs* upon that and other Sacred Actions in our Churches, *too Horrible* to be repeated.

If they take away from us, one of the *Songs* among the Ancient *Jews,* they would however leave us room for one of the *Sighs* uttered by a *Rabby* among them; *The worst Fruit which we Eat in our Youth, Excelled the best which we now Eat in our Old Age, for in our days the World is changed.*

6. Concerning all Sinful Attempts to overturn the *Order of the Gospel,* hitherto upheld in the Churches of *New-England* and to spoil that Glorious *Work* of God, which we have seen him doing, with a *Series of Remarkable Providences,* in erecting such *Congregational Churches* in these ends of the Earth; We would now therefore bear our *Testimony,* that they are doubtless Displeasing to our Lord Jesus Christ, who *walks in the midst of these Golden Candlesticks,* and they will prove *Bitterness in the latter End.*

And this we Declare with the more concern upon our minds, because of an observation, so plain, that *he that runs may Read it.*

It is too observable, that the *Power of Godliness,* is exceedingly Decaying and Expiring ill the Country; and one great point in the Decay of the Tower of Godliness, is men's growing weary of the *Congregational Church-Discipline,* which is evidently Calculated for to maintain it.

If that *Church-Discipline* were more thoroughly and vigorously kept alive, even by those that make profession of it, it might be hoped, that the Lord would Sanctify it, for the Revival of *all Godliness* in the Land.

But if this *Church-Discipline* come to be given up, we think it our Duty, to leave this *Warning* with the Churches, that probably the *Apostasy* will not *Stop there:* For the same Spirit that will dispose the next Generation to change their way, in one point, will dispose them to more, and more *changes* (even in *Doctrine* and *Worship* as well as in *Manners*) until it may be feared, *the Candlestick will quickly be removed out of its place.*

7. We do therefore Humbly propose it, unto all the Churches, as a great *Expedient,* for the preservation of our *Church-State,* that more Prayer (even in whole *days of Prayer* set apart for that end) with other *appointed means,* may be used in the Churches to obtain from the Lord, the *Outpourings of the Spirit of Grace on the Rising Generation.* If so Rich a Blessing were obtained, (and our *Heavenly Father*

will give his Holy Spirit unto them that ask it,) and if the *Rising Generation* might be a Praying, Pious, Devout and *Regenerate Generation*, there will not be much danger as now there is, of their *Easily giving away* the precious *Legacy* which their Father's (now beholding the Face of the Lord Jesus Christ in Glory,) left unto them, or of their Doting upon *Innovations* Fatal to the *Order of the Gospel* among us.

8. Now as Aged *Joseph* said, *I Dy, and God will surely visit you;* Even so, we the unworthy Servants of the Lord, whose Age bids us every day look for Death, and our Call to that World, *where to be is by far the best of all,* do Conclude with our Prayers unto the Lord for these Holy Churches, that He would *Surely visit* them, and Grant much of His Gracious *Presence* and *Spirit* in the midst of them; and Raise up from time to time, those who may be Happy instruments of *bringing down the Hearts of the Parents into the Children.* The Lord Bless these His Churches, and keep them *Steadfast,* both in *the Faith and in the Order of the Gospel, and be with them, as he was with their Fathers, and never leave them nor forsake them.*

John Higginton
William Hubbard

Postscript

That our Testimony to the Old Principles of New-England may be the more (Jiftinctiy apprehended, we recommend unto Consideration, three Pages in the Life of Mr. John Cotton, written by his Grand-Son, Mr. Cotton Mather. p. 33, 34, 35.

NOW that the World may know, *The First Principles of* NEW ENGLAND, it must be known that until the *Platform of Church Discipline* Published by a *Synod* in the year 1648. next unto the Bible which was the professed, perpetual, and only *Directory* of these Churches they had no *Platform* of their Church Government, more Exact than their Famous John Cotton's well known Book of *The Keys;* which Book, endeavours to lay out, the Just *Lines* and *Bounds,* of all *Church Power,* and so defines the matter; That as in the State, there is a

Dispersion of Powers into several Hands, which are to *concur* into all Acts of *common concernment;* from whence arises the Healthy Constitution of a Common-Wealth: In like sort, he assigns the Powers in the Church, unto several Subjects, wherein the United light of Scripture and of *Nature,* have placed them with a very Satisfactory Distribution.

He asserts, That a Presbyterated Society of the Faithful, hath within itself, a compleat Power of Self-Reformation, or if you will, of Self-Preservation, and may within it self, manage its own Choices of *Officers,* and *Censures of Delinquents.* Now a special *Statute-Law* of our Lord, having excepted *Women* and *Children,* from enjoying any part of this Power, he finds only *Elders* and *Brethren* to be the *Constituent Members,* who may Act in such a *Sacred Corporation;* the Elders he finds the *First Subject* entrusted with *Government;* the *Brethren* endowed with Privilege, in so much that though the *Elders* are to *Rule* the Church, and without them there can be no *Elections, Admissions,* or *Excommunications,* and they have a *Negative* upon the *Acts* of the *Fraternity*, as well as 'tis *they only* that have the Power of *Authoritative Preaching* and Administering the Sacraments: Yet the *Brethren* have such a *Liberty* that without *Their* Consent, nothing of Common Concernment may be Imposed upon them. Nevertheless, because *Particular Churches* of *Elders* and *Brethren* may abuse their *Powers,* with manifold miscarriages, he Asserts the Necessary *Communion of Churches* in *Synods,* who have Authority to Determine, Declare and Enjoyn, such things as may Rectify the *Male-Administrations,* of any Disorders, Dissentions and Confusions of the *Congregations* which fall under their Cognizance. But still so as Co leave unto the *Particular* Churches themselves, the *Formal Acts,* which are to be done pursuant unto the Advice of the *Council;* upon the Scandalous and obstinate Refusal whereof, the *Council* may Determine to *withdraw Communion* from them, as from those who will not be counselled, against a *Notorious Mismanagement* of the *Jurisdiction* which the Lord Jesus Christ has given them. This was the *Design* of that *Judicious Treatise,* wherein vas contained the substance of our Church-*Discipline,* and whereof we have one Remarkable thing to Relate as we go along. That Great Person, who afterwards proved one of the Greatest Scholars, Divines and Writers in this Age, then under Prejudices of conversation, set himself to write a *Confutation* of this very Treatise, *of the*

Keys; but having made a considerable Progress in his undertaking, such was the strength of this *Unanswerable Book,* that instead of confuting it, it conquered hi*m;* and this *Book of the Keys,* was happily so Blessed of God for the *conveyance* of *Congregational Principles* into the now *Opened mind* of this Learned man, that^ he not only wrote in Defence of Mr. Cotton, but also exposed himself to more than a little Sorrow and Labour all his days, for the maintaining of those principles. Upon which occasion the words of the Doctor [*Owen,* in his *Review of the true Nature of Schism*] are, *This way of Impartial Examining all things by the Word, and laying aside all prejudicate Respect unto persons, or present Traditions, is a course that I would Admonish all to beware of, who would avoid the danger of being made* (what they call) *Independents.* Having said thus much, of that Book, all that we shall add concerning it, is, That the Eminent Mr. *Rutherford* himself, in his Treatise Entitled, *A Survey of the Spiritual Antichrist,* has these words, *Mr.* Cotton in his *Treatise of the Keys of the Kingdom of Heaven, is well found in our way; if he had given some more Power to Assemblies, and in some letter points.*

John Higginson.
William Hubbard.

FINIS